W9-AXX-099

# Table of Contents

# Introduction

Types of stories:
- Folk Tales
- Fairy Tales
- Realistic Fiction
- Nonfiction
- Poetry

Stories span from mid-first to beginning third grade reading levels and can be used in several ways:

1. As directed lessons
   - with small groups of students reading at the same level
   - with an individual student

2. For partner reading

3. For independent practice
   - at school
   - at home

Determine your purpose for selecting a story—instructional device, partner reading, or independent reading. Each purpose calls for a different degree of story difficulty.

A single story can be used for more than one purpose. You might first use the story as an instructional tool, have partners read the story a second time for greater fluency, and then use it at a later time for independent reading.

When presenting a story to a group or individual student, discuss any vocabulary that might be difficult to decode or understand.

Each story is followed by five pages of activities covering a variety of reading skills:

- Comprehension—recall story details, draw conclusions, make inferences & predictions, sequence events
- Vocabulary
- Phonics
- Word Attack—compound words, suffixes, contractions, syllables
- Parts of speech—nouns, verbs, adjectives, pronouns
- Record information—list, categorize

The questions relating to drawing conclusions and making inferences and predictions always occur at the end of the list of questions. If you feel any of these questions are too difficult for your students, cover them before reproducing the page.

Several students may read the same story but need to practice different skills. Provide each reader with the task that is appropriate for his/her needs.

Skill pages can be used more than once.

1. As directed mini-lessons with a small group or individual student:

   • Make a transparency for students to follow as you work through the lesson.

   • Write the activity on the chalkboard and call on students to fill in the answers as a group.

   • Reproduce the page for everyone to use as you go through the lesson.

2. As independent practice:

   Independent practice should be on skills already introduced to the reader. Review directions and be sure the student understands what is to be done. Go over the completed assignment with the student to determine if further practice is needed.

# Max and the Funny Fox

Max and Uncle Ted had spent the afternoon fishing. Now Uncle Ted was building a campfire to cook the day's catch.

"Max, will you get my jacket?" called Uncle Ted. "I left it in the tent." Max ran over to the tent to get the jacket.

"Didn't we shut the tent flap?" asked Max. "Why is it open now?" He peeked inside. The tent was a mess!

"Uncle Ted, come quick!" yelled Max. "Someone's been in the tent." Just then Max saw that his sleeping bag was wiggling. The next thing he saw was a little red head peeking out of the bag. It was a fox! Max began to laugh. The little fox had one of his sox in its mouth.

Uncle Ted pulled Max out of the tent. He opened the flap wide and stood back. The little fox made a quick exit.

Max and Uncle Ted picked up the mess. Then Uncle Ted tied the tent flap shut.

"We don't want any more animal visitors," he laughed. "Now, let's go cook those fish."

Read and Understand Grade 2 EMC 639

Name _____

## Questions About *Max and the Funny Fox*

1. Where had Max and Uncle Ted been?

   _____

2. What did Max see when he got to the tent?

   _____

3. What had made the big mess inside the tent?

   _____

4. How did Max know something was in the sleeping bag?

   _____

5. What made Max laugh?

   _____

6. Why did Uncle Ted pull Max out of the tent?

   _____

7. Why did Uncle Ted tie the flap of the tent shut?

   _____

8. Why do you think the fox went into the tent?

   _____

Name _____

Cut out the sentences.
Paste them in order.

1. 

2. 

3. 

4. 

5. 

6. 

The inside of the tent was a mess.

The fox ran out of the tent.

Uncle Ted asked Max to get his jacket.

A fox peeked out of the sleeping bag.

Max saw that the tent flap was open.

Uncle Ted pulled Max out of the tent.

Name _____

# What Does It Mean?

**Match:**

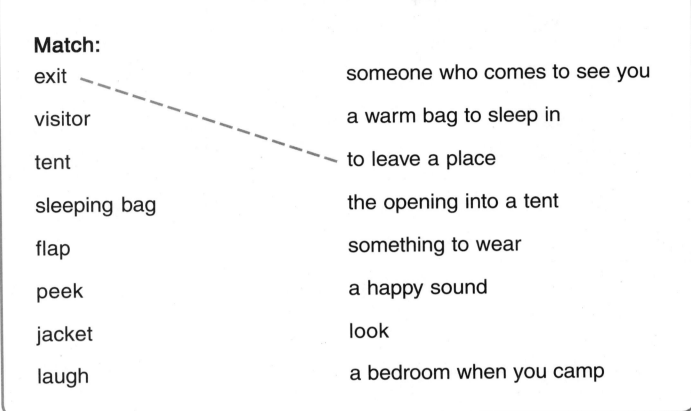

| | |
|---|---|
| exit | someone who comes to see you |
| visitor | a warm bag to sleep in |
| tent | to leave a place |
| sleeping bag | the opening into a tent |
| flap | something to wear |
| peek | a happy sound |
| jacket | look |
| laugh | a bedroom when you camp |

Write the words for each picture.

_____  _____  _____

     Read and Understand Grade 2 EMC 639

Name _____

## The Letter X

Write the name.

| | | |
|---|---|---|
| _____ | _____ | _____ |
| _____ | _____ | _____ |

## OO Sounds

Read these words.
Write them under the words they rhyme with.

took        hood        moon        stood
hoop        bloom       book        wood
shook       boot        school      food

| noon | | cook | |
|---|---|---|---|
| _____ | _____ | _____ | _____ |
| _____ | _____ | _____ | _____ |
| _____ | _____ | _____ | _____ |

Name _____

## X Crossword Puzzle

**Word Box**
exit
fix
fox
Max
mix
next

**Across**
3. to go out
4. a name
5. small animal

**Down**
1. come after
2. repair
4. stir

## What Do You See?

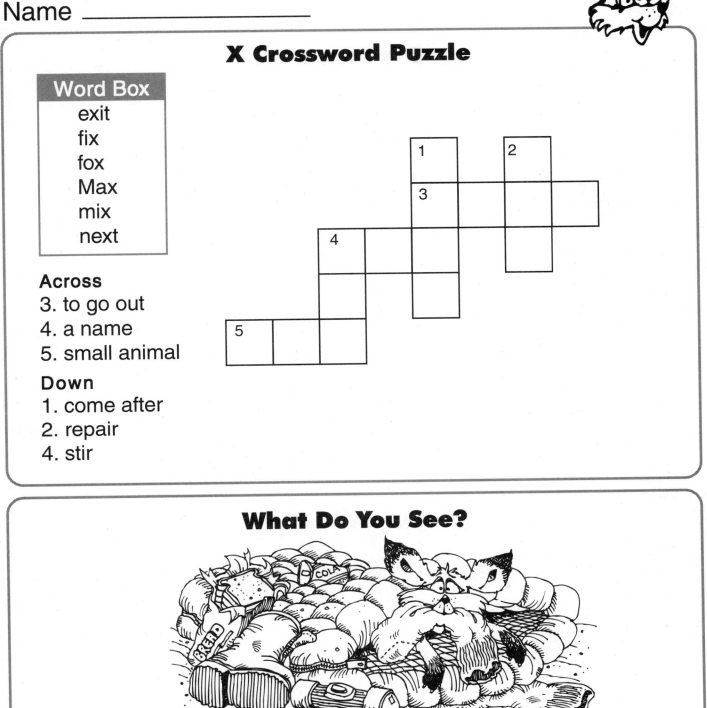

The fox is in a _____.

It has one of Max's _____ in its mouth.

The fox ripped open _____.

# Bugs!

"Eeek! A bug!" shouted Susan.

"I'm not a bug. I'm a grasshopper," said a tiny, little voice.

"I jump high and far on my strong back legs."

"Eeek! A bug!" yelled Yolanda.

"I'm not a bug. I'm a beetle," said a tiny, little voice.

"My wings are protected by a shiny hard cover."

"Eeek! A bug!" cried Carlos.

"I'm not a bug. I'm a cricket," said a tiny, little voice.

"I rub my wings together to make a chirping sound."

"Eeek! A bug!" howled Harry.

"I'm not a bug. I'm a bumblebee," said a tiny, little voice.

"I fly from flower to flower collecting pollen to take back to my hive."

"Then what is a bug?" asked Susan, Yolanda, Carlos, and Harry.

"I'm a bug," said a tiny, little voice. "I look a lot like a beetle," said the bug, "but I eat in a different way. I have a long tube I use to suck juice from my food.

"Remember," explained the bug, "a bug is an insect, but not all insects are bugs."

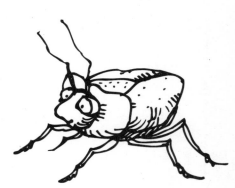

Name _____

## Questions About *Bugs!*

1. What did the children do when they saw insects?

   _____

2. What can these insects do?

   grasshopper _____

   bumblebee _____

   cricket _____

3. How does a beetle protect its wings?

   _____

4. How is a bug different than a beetle?

   _____

5. Would you say "Eeek!" if you saw a bug? Why?

   _____

   _____

Draw your favorite insect.

Name _____

## Name the Insects

Write the insects in the order the children saw them.
Tell who saw the insect.

1. _____ _____

2. _____ _____

3. _____ _____

4. _____ _____

5. _____ _____

## What Goes Together?

Cut out the words.
Write them in the correct box.

| Insects | People | Plants |
|---|---|---|
| _____ | _____ | _____ |
| _____ | _____ | _____ |
| _____ | _____ | _____ |
| _____ | _____ | _____ |
| _____ | _____ | _____ |

| | | |
|---|---|---|
| Susan | bush | Harry |
| grasshopper | ant | bug |
| tree | moth | weed |
| Carlos | vine | cricket |
| Maria | flower | Yolanda |

Name _____

## What Did I Say?

Read the story.
Circle words that mean the same thing as *said*.
Write the words here.

The bug ___*said*___          Susan _____

Yolanda _____          Carlos _____

Harry _____          The bug _____

## Crossword Puzzle

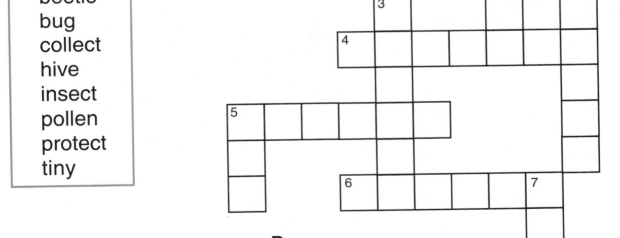

**Word Box**
beetle
bug
collect
hive
insect
pollen
protect
tiny

**Across**

4. pick up
5. insect with hard wing covers
6. what a grasshopper or cricket is

**Down**

1. a bee home
2. keep from danger
3. yellow powder collected by bees
5. a kind of insect
7. very small

13                    Read and Understand Grade 2 EMC 639

Name _____

# What Does the Letter Say?

Write the letter you hear at the end of each word.

cry ___i___     happy ___e___

1. my _____          6. tummy _____

2. shy _____          7. fly _____

3. tiny _____          8. silly _____

4. pretty _____        9. many _____

5. funny _____        10. by _____

What sound do you hear at the end of the two-syllable words? _____

What sound do you hear at the end of the one-syllable words? _____

# Counting Syllables

Color the insects.

one syllable—red     two syllables—green     three syllables—orange

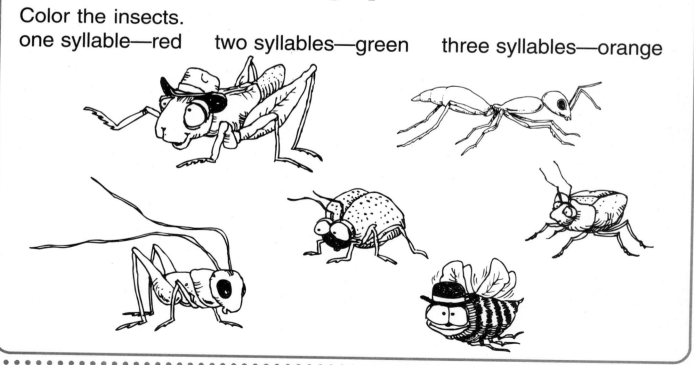

Name _____

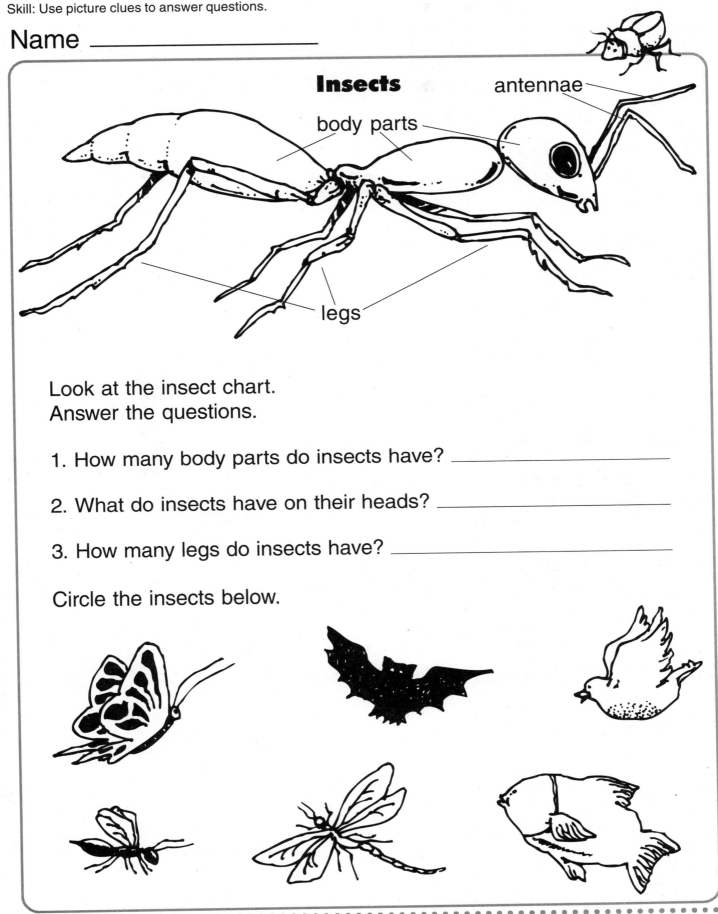

**Insects**

antennae

body parts

legs

Look at the insect chart.
Answer the questions.

1. How many body parts do insects have? _____

2. What do insects have on their heads? _____

3. How many legs do insects have? _____

Circle the insects below.

# A Message from Uncle Wilber

Our Uncle Wilber is a little strange. We can never tell what he will send us. Last week there was a knock at the door. When the messenger gave us a box, we knew it had to be from Uncle Wilber. It was full of holes and covered with messages.

"What do you think it is this time?" I asked my sister.

"I know it's something strange," Sarah said.

We opened the box. Inside was a goldfish in a bowl and a letter. The letter said...

> Dear Sarah and Sid,
> This is Oscar, my pet goldfish.
> Please take good care of him while I am away.
> Talk to him. He likes it.
> See you next week.
>                    Love,
>                    Uncle Wilber

On Friday Uncle Wilber came to take Oscar home. We'll miss him, but Uncle Wilber left us a thank-you present. This box is full of holes. It is covered with messages. The box is very heavy. It hisses too.

"I don't know if I want to open it," whispered Sid.

"I'll do it," said Sarah. Slowly she undid the knot and lifted off the lid.

"Eeeeek!"

Name _____

# Questions About *A Message from Uncle Wilber*

1. What did the messenger bring Sarah and Sid?

   _____

2. Why did Uncle Wilber send Oscar to Sarah and Sid?

   _____

3. How long did they take care of Oscar?

   _____

4. What did Uncle Wilber give Sarah and Sid as a thank-you gift?

   _____

5. What do you think would happen if Sid or Sarah poked a finger into a hole in the box?

   _____

   _____

6. Why did Sarah and Sid think Uncle Wilber was a little strange?

   _____

Draw what you think is in the thank-you present from Uncle Wilber.

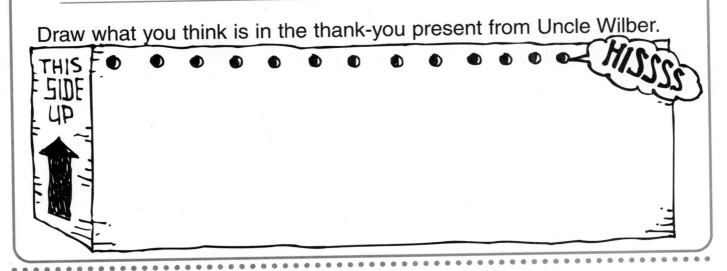

Name _____

# What Happened Next?

Cut out the sentences.
Paste them in order.

There was a knock at the door.

1. |                                                      |
2. |                                                      |
3. |                                                      |
4. |                                                      |
5. |                                                      |
6. |                                                      |

Eeeek!

| Sarah and Sid took care of Oscar. |

| Something in the box hissed. |

| A messenger came with a box. |

| Uncle Wilber came on Friday. |

| A goldfish in a bowl was in the box. |

| Uncle Wilber left a thank-you present. |

# Name _____

## What Does It Mean?

Match:

messenger                 words sent from one person to another

message                   a tap on the door

strange                   a present

knock                     a person that brings messages

gift                      different

## Warnings

The boxes in the story had warnings.
Read these warnings.
Write them on the signs.

                wet paint          this side up
                stop               keep off the grass

Name _____

## Not a Sound

When you read **kn,** the **k** does not make a sound.
You say just the sound of **n**.

<u>kn</u>ow        <u>kn</u>ew        <u>kn</u>ock

Each of these pictures is a kn word. Write the picture names on the lines. Then tell a friend a sentence that uses one of the words.

knob        knee        knot
knit        knife        knight

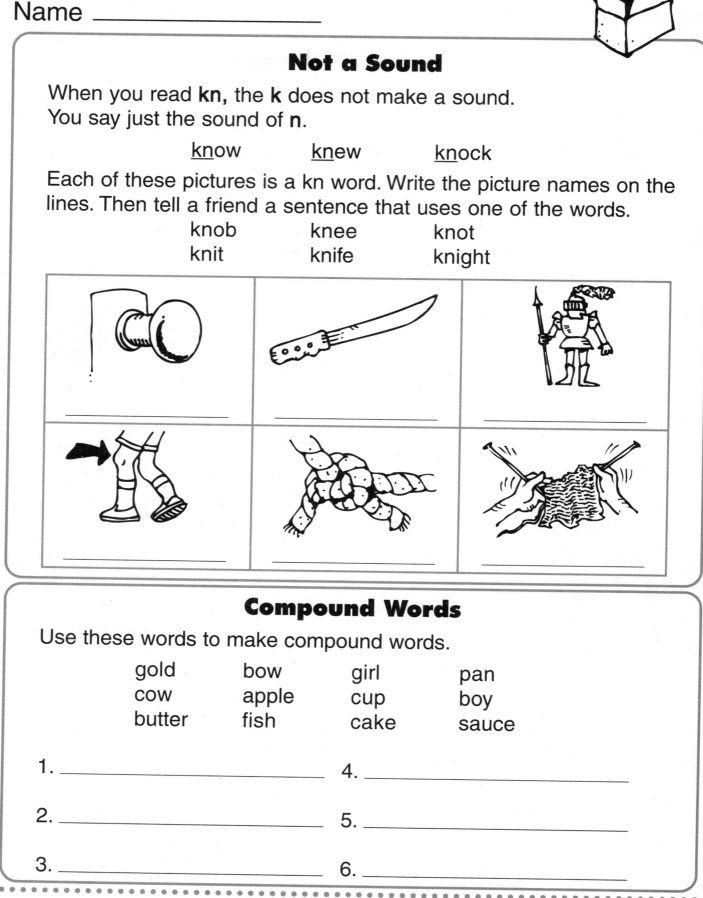

## Compound Words

Use these words to make compound words.

gold        bow        girl        pan
cow        apple        cup        boy
butter        fish        cake        sauce

1. _____        4. _____

2. _____        5. _____

3. _____        6. _____

Read and Understand Grade 2 EMC 639

Name _____

## Bonnie's Birthday

Look at the picture. Read what Bonnie is saying.
Color in the circle to answer the question.

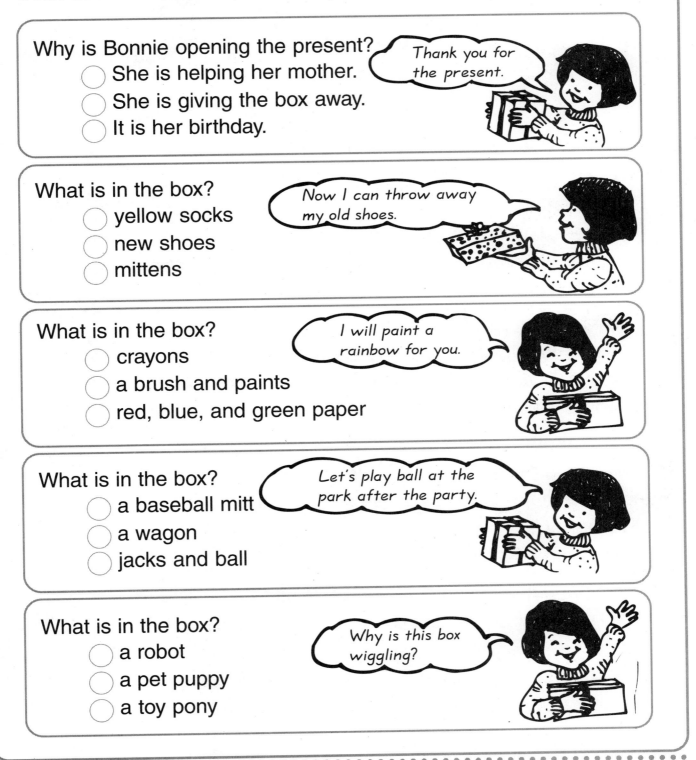

Why is Bonnie opening the present?
○ She is helping her mother.
○ She is giving the box away.
○ It is her birthday.

*Thank you for the present.*

What is in the box?
○ yellow socks
○ new shoes
○ mittens

*Now I can throw away my old shoes.*

What is in the box?
○ crayons
○ a brush and paints
○ red, blue, and green paper

*I will paint a rainbow for you.*

What is in the box?
○ a baseball mitt
○ a wagon
○ jacks and ball

*Let's play ball at the park after the party.*

What is in the box?
○ a robot
○ a pet puppy
○ a toy pony

*Why is this box wiggling?*

Read and Understand Grade 2 EMC 639

# The Giant Carrot

Grandfather liked to work in his garden. He grew rows and rows of the vegetable he liked most—carrots.

Grandfather saw that one carrot was much bigger than the rest. The green top of the carrot was as tall as Grandfather. He grabbed it and pulled. He pulled very hard. The giant carrot would not come out.

Grandfather called Grandmother and asked her to help. Grandmother came to the garden. She pulled on Grandfather. Grandfather pulled on the carrot top. The giant carrot would not come out.

Grandmother called her pet cat and asked it to help. The pet cat came to the garden. He pulled on Grandmother. Grandmother pulled on Grandfather. Grandfather pulled on the carrot top. The giant carrot would not come out.

The pet cat called to a little gray mouse and asked it to help. The little gray mouse came to the garden. It pulled on the pet cat. The pet cat pulled on Grandmother. Grandmother pulled on Grandfather. Grandfather pulled on the carrot top. They pulled and pulled and pulled...

**and the carrot came out!**

Read and Understand Grade 2 EMC 639

Skills: Recall details from a story; make predictions.

Name ____________________

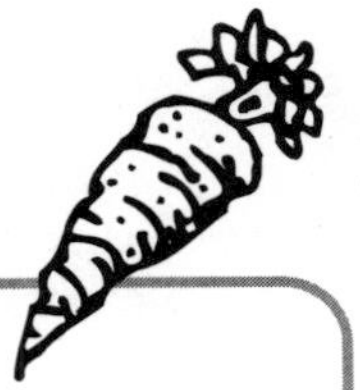

## Questions About *The Giant Carrot*

1. Where did Grandfather like to work?

________________________________________

2. What did he grow in the garden?

________________________________________

3. What was Grandfather's problem?

________________________________________

4. How did Grandfather get the giant carrot out of the ground?

________________________________________

________________________________________

5. What do you think Grandfather will do with the giant carrot?

________________________________________

Draw a picture of a carrot growing in the garden.

| |
|---|
| on top<br>of the<br>ground |
| under<br>the<br>ground |

Name _____

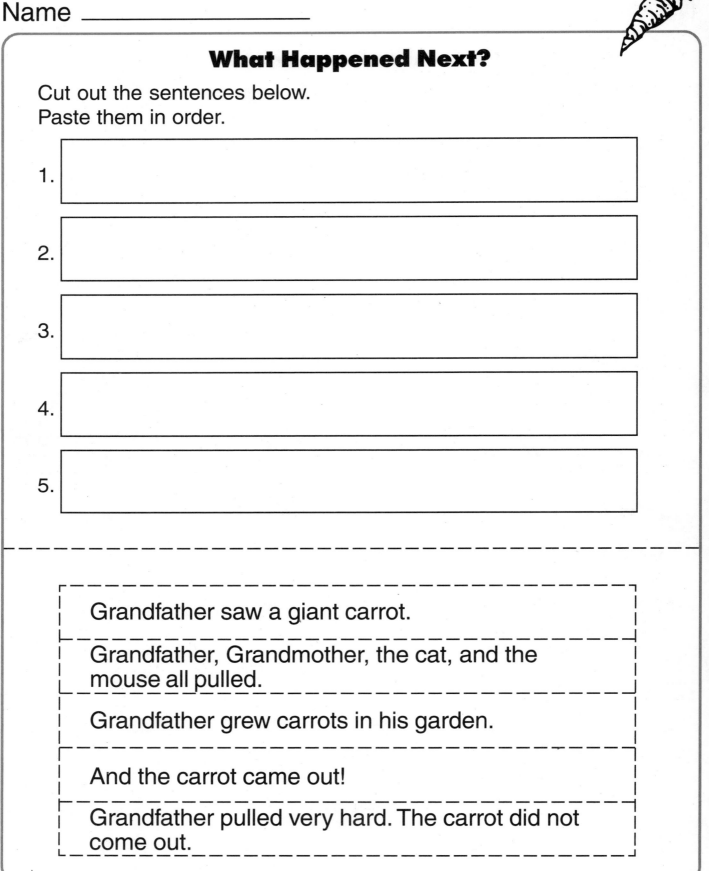

## What Happened Next?

Cut out the sentences below.
Paste them in order.

1.

2.

3.

4.

5.

---

Grandfather saw a giant carrot.

Grandfather, Grandmother, the cat, and the mouse all pulled.

Grandfather grew carrots in his garden.

And the carrot came out!

Grandfather pulled very hard. The carrot did not come out.

Name _____

## Vegetable Garden

Answer the riddles to find the vegetables in the garden.

|          |          |          |
|----------|----------|----------|
| beet     | peas     | corn     |
| celery   | carrot   | spinach  |

| 1. We are little, round, and green. | 2. I'm yellow, sweet and good to eat. | 3. I'm red and round. I grow under the ground. |
|---|---|---|
| _____ | _____ | _____ |
| 4. I'm long and orange with a green top. | 5. My green leaves are good to eat. | 6. Eat my long, crunchy stems. |
| _____ | _____ | _____ |

Now, read this list of vegetables.
Find them in the puzzle.

_____ beet            _____ peas

✔ broccoli            _____ potato

_____ carrot          _____ radish

_____ corn            _____ spinach

_____ eggplant        _____ squash

_____ green beans     _____ turnip

```
b r o c c o l i c x c s
e g g p l a n t o p a p
e t u r n i p z r e r i
t w s q u a s h n a r n
g r e e n b e a n s o a
p o t a t o b a l l t c
a p p l e r a d i s h h
```

Skills: Review short vowel sounds; identify nouns.

Name ____________________

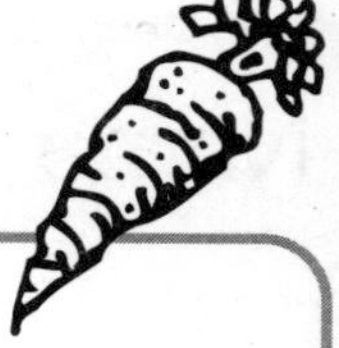

## Vowels

Circle the words that have these short vowel sounds.

a - at     e - egg     i - in     o - on     u - up

| | | |
|---|---|---|
| Tom | pull | car |
| had | egg | pick |
| to | the | tug |
| fill | ten | apple |
| are | see | is |
| mine | up | hot |
| ask | beg | over |
| under | off | mule |

## What's My Name?

Read the story.

Circle the words that name things. Write the names here.

carrot ____________________     ____________________

____________________     ____________________

____________________     ____________________

____________________     ____________________

These words are called nouns.

Skill: Record personal information.

Name ____________________

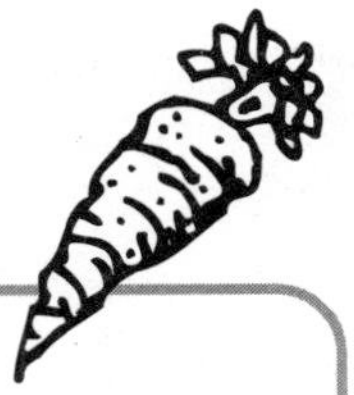

## My Favorite Vegetable

Grandfather liked carrots most.
What vegetable do you like best?

I like ____________________ best.

Why? ______________________________________________

______________________________________________

Draw it here.

# The Three Billy Goats Gruff

Once upon a time there was a family of billy goats named Gruff. The three goats lived on a hill near a wide river. Every day the goats looked across the river at the tall, green grass growing on a hillside.

"That grass looks so tasty," said the littlest Billy Goat Gruff.

"It must taste better than our grass," said the second Billy Goat Gruff.

"It's not safe to go across the bridge," warned the biggest Billy Goat Gruff. He knew a bad troll lived under the bridge. The troll had big eyes and a long crooked nose, and he liked to eat goats more than anything in the world.

Read and Understand Grade 2 EMC 639

One day the littlest Billy Goat Gruff went down the trail to the bridge. He just had to have some of that tall, green grass. As the little goat started across the bridge, out jumped the troll. "I'm going to eat you up!" growled the troll.

"I'm too little. Wait for my brother. He is bigger," begged the little goat. So the troll did.

The next day the second Billy Goat Gruff went down the trail to the bridge. As he started across the bridge, out jumped the troll again. The troll shouted, "I'm going to eat you up!"

"I'm too little. Wait for my brother. He is much bigger," said the second goat. So the troll did. At last the biggest Billy Goat Gruff went down the trail to the bridge. As he started across, the troll jumped out one more time, shouting, "I'm going to eat you up!"

"Come up and try," roared Big Billy Goat Gruff. So the troll did. Big Billy Goat Gruff hit the troll so hard that he was never seen again. Now every day the three goats go over the bridge to the hillside to eat grass.

Skills: Recall story details; draw conclusions; distinguish between real and make-believe elements.

## Name _____

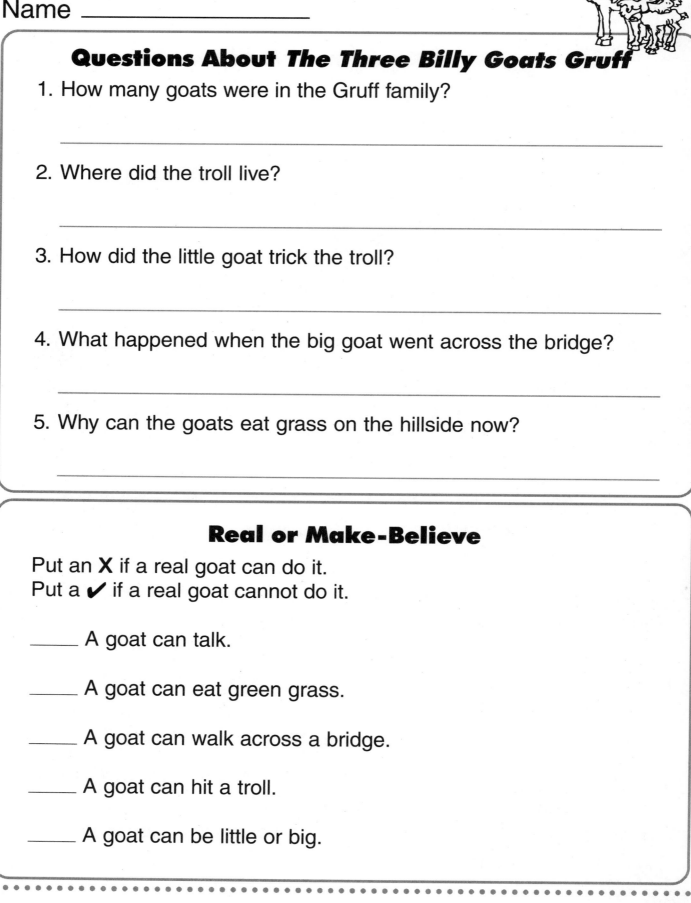

# Questions About *The Three Billy Goats Gruff*

1. How many goats were in the Gruff family?

   _____

2. Where did the troll live?

   _____

3. How did the little goat trick the troll?

   _____

4. What happened when the big goat went across the bridge?

   _____

5. Why can the goats eat grass on the hillside now?

   _____

# Real or Make-Believe

Put an **X** if a real goat can do it.
Put a ✔ if a real goat cannot do it.

_____ A goat can talk.

_____ A goat can eat green grass.

_____ A goat can walk across a bridge.

_____ A goat can hit a troll.

_____ A goat can be little or big.

Name _____

## What Happened Next?

Number the pictures in order to tell the story.

Name _____

# What Does It Mean?

Write the word by its meaning.
You will not use all the words.

| | | |
|---|---|---|
| family | bridge | growl |
| crooked | second | hillside |
| across | beg | troll |

1. something built over a river so people can go across _____

2. bent or twisted _____

3. ask for something _____

4. an ugly creature in fairy tales _____

5. comes after first _____

6. an angry sound used as a warning _____

# Match the Parts

The goats ate grass          to eat the goats.

A bad troll wanted          across the bridge.

The goats went          on the hillside.

"Try to eat me,"          said Big Billy Goat Gruff.

The troll jumped out          said the little goat.

"Wait for my brother,"          and shouted at the goat.

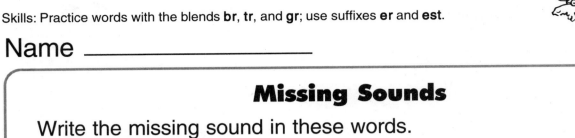

Name _____

## Missing Sounds

Write the missing sound in these words.

br          tr          gr

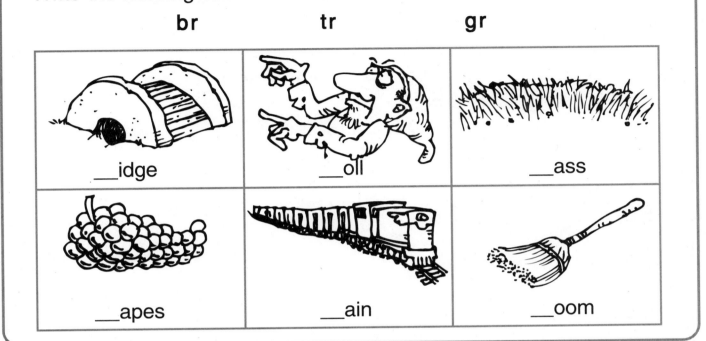

___idge        ___oll        ___ass

___apes        ___ain        ___oom

## Word Endings

Write the ending.

1. Jack is tall____ than his brother.

2. That is the tall___ tree in the park.

3. The orange pumpkin is the
   bigg___ one I ever saw.

4. Snow is cold___ than rain.

5. That is the fast___ horse I ever rode.

biggest  bigger  big

Name _____

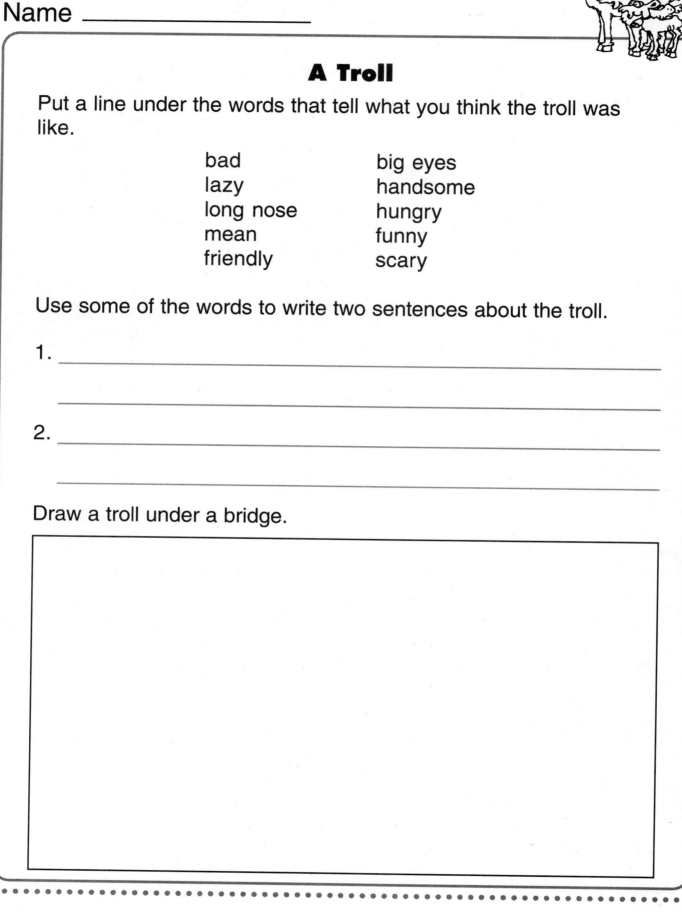

# A Troll

Put a line under the words that tell what you think the troll was like.

| | |
|---|---|
| bad | big eyes |
| lazy | handsome |
| long nose | hungry |
| mean | funny |
| friendly | scary |

Use some of the words to write two sentences about the troll.

1. _____

_____

2. _____

_____

Draw a troll under a bridge.

# Cary's Hamster

Cary has a pet of his very own. It is small and furry. It has twitchy whiskers and little black eyes. Can you guess what it is? You're right. It's a little hamster.

Cary named his hamster Hammy. He takes good care of his pet. He knows Hammy needs a good place to live. Hammy has a cage with a lot of room. There is even a little hamster house for him to sleep in. Cary keeps Hammy's cage clean.

Cary gives his pet water and good things to eat. He feeds Hammy dry pet food made for hamsters. Hammy likes fruit, vegetables, seeds, and tiny bits of raw hamburger too. He stuffs food in his cheeks and takes it into his house. He will eat it later. Cary likes to watch Hammy eat.

Hamsters need things to play with. Cary put a wheel and tubes in the cage. Hammy runs around his cage. He plays on the wheel and he crawls through the tubes. Hammy likes to tear up bits of paper too.

Cary knows not to wake Hammy up when he is sleeping. He knows not to play with Hammy too long at a time. Even a tame hamster like Hammy will bite if it is scared or tired.

Cary's parents say he takes such good care of Hammy that he can have another pet. What do you think that pet will be?

Read and Understand Grade 2 EMC 639

Name _____

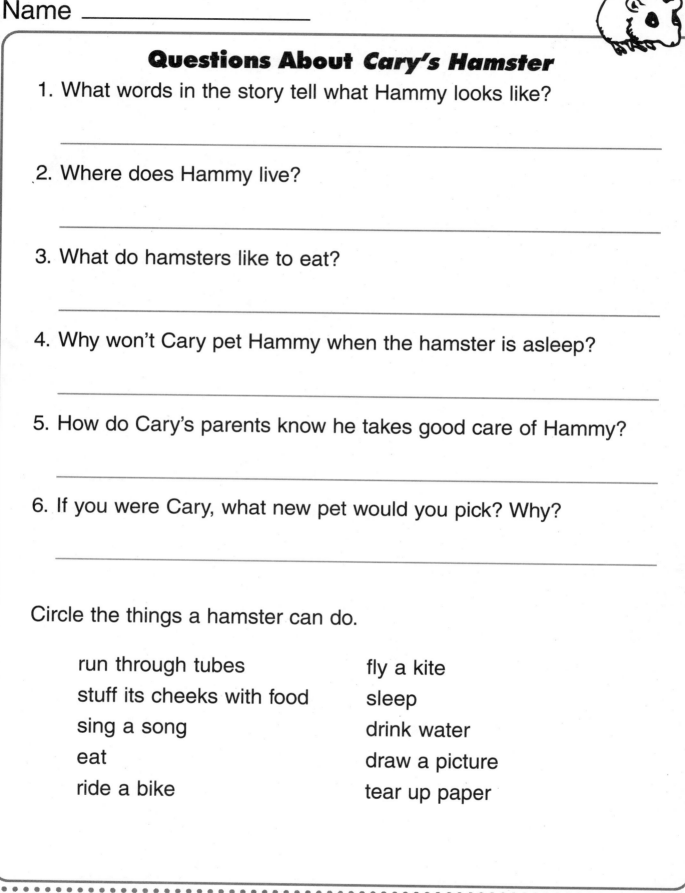

## Questions About *Cary's Hamster*

1. What words in the story tell what Hammy looks like?

   _____

2. Where does Hammy live?

   _____

3. What do hamsters like to eat?

   _____

4. Why won't Cary pet Hammy when the hamster is asleep?

   _____

5. How do Cary's parents know he takes good care of Hammy?

   _____

6. If you were Cary, what new pet would you pick? Why?

   _____

Circle the things a hamster can do.

| | |
|---|---|
| run through tubes | fly a kite |
| stuff its cheeks with food | sleep |
| sing a song | drink water |
| eat | draw a picture |
| ride a bike | tear up paper |

Name _____

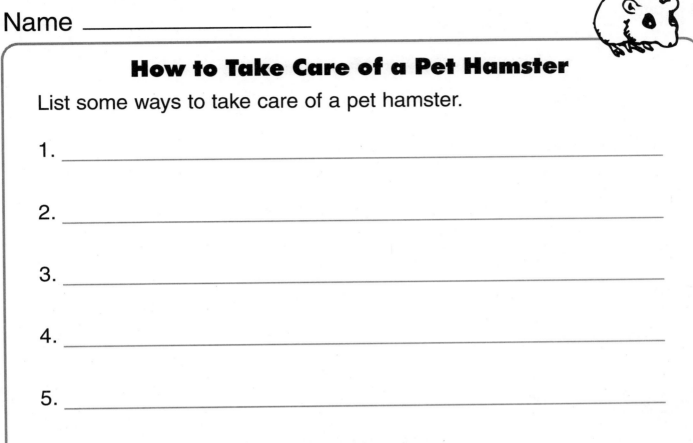

# How to Take Care of a Pet Hamster

List some ways to take care of a pet hamster.

1. _____

2. _____

3. _____

4. _____

5. _____

Draw a pet hamster in its cage. Show what the hamster needs.

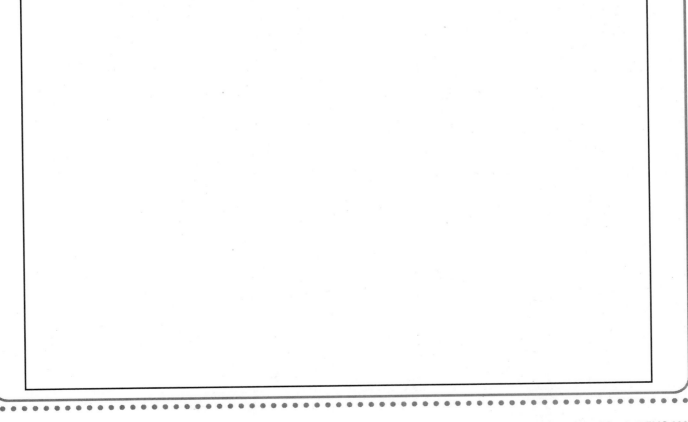

Name _____

# Hammy, the Hamster

Read the story again to find the answers.

1. Hammy is a _____.

2. He lives in a _____.

3. He has _____ whiskers.

4. He eats small bits of raw _____.

5. He likes to _____ paper.

6. He runs around on a _____.

## Crossword Puzzle

### Word Box
cage
furry
hamster
raw
tame
twitchy
wheel
whiskers

**Across**

2. a pen for a small pet
4. long hairs on the sides of a hamster's face
5. a small furry pet
7. a round frame that turns
8. very hairy

**Down**

1. not wild
3. wiggly
6. not cooked

Name _____

## Silent E

An **e** at the end of a word can make the vowel sound long.

can + e = cane     tub + e = tube

Circle the missing word.

| | | |
|---|---|---|
| 1. I took a big _____ of cookie. | bit | bite |
| 2. Nan opened a _____ of food for her cat. | can | cane |
| 3. Did you have a birthday _____? | cak | cake |
| 4. Lonnie took a little _____ of the clay. | bit | bite |
| 5. Grandpa has a _____ to help him walk. | can | cane |
| 6. The hamster is kept in a _____. | cag | cage |
| 7. We take baths in a _____. | tub | tube |
| 8. The cowboy had to _____ the wild horse. | tam | tame |

## Sounds of C

Read the words.
Write the sound you hear **c** make (k or s).

1. cage    _____k_____          6. mice    _____

2. face    _____s_____          7. cent    _____

3. place    _____           8. picnic    _____

4. coat    _____           9. candy    _____

5. bacon    _____          10. city    _____

Name _____

# Hamsters

1. Draw a circle around the hamster eating an apple slice.
2. Color the biggest hamster brown.
3. Color the smallest hamster black.
4. Draw a box around the hamster running on the wheel.
5. Put an X on the hamster with food stuffed in its cheeks.
6. Draw a hamster inside the little house.

40

# Maggie's Kite

Hi! My name's Maggie. I have always wanted a kite. I didn't want one that you buy at the store. I wanted a kite I made all by myself. This spring I made one.

Mom said I had to earn the money to buy the stuff I needed. For two weeks I worked. I mowed the lawn. I baby-sat my little brother. I even gave the dog a bath.

At last I had all the money I needed. I ran to the craft shop to get paper, wood, glue, and kite string.

I had to think a long time about just the right way to make it. Then I went to work. My little brother kept wanting to help. So I locked myself in my room until the kite was finished.

This morning the kite was done. Boy, it looked great! After lunch I raced to the park to try it out. The wind was just right. I took a running start and up the kite went soaring high into the sky.

That's my kite up there. The torn one caught on that tree branch. This has been a terrible day!

Read and Understand Grade 2 EMC 639

Name _____

## Questions About *Maggie's Kite*

1. What kind of kite did Maggie want?

_____

2. What "stuff" did Maggie buy to make the kite?

_____

3. Why did Maggie have to lock her door?

_____

4. How do you think the kite got caught on the tree branch?

_____

5. How did Maggie feel when her kite hit the tree?

_____

6. What do you think will happen next?

_____

## How Did Maggie Feel?

Circle the face to show how Maggie felt.

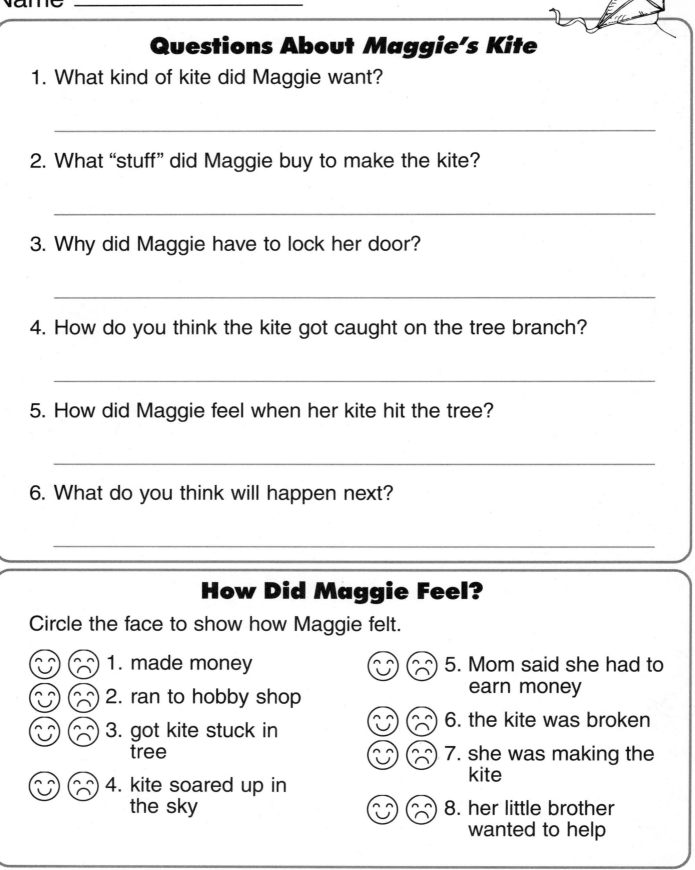

1. made money
2. ran to hobby shop
3. got kite stuck in tree
4. kite soared up in the sky
5. Mom said she had to earn money
6. the kite was broken
7. she was making the kite
8. her little brother wanted to help

Name _____

# What Happened Next?

Draw to show what happened next.

Name _____

# What Does It Mean?

Circle the letter.

1. How did Maggie move when she **raced** to the park?
   a. ran very fast
   b. walked quickly
   c. drove a car

2. What can you buy at a **craft shop**?
   a. something to eat
   b. a new hat
   c. the stuff you need to make things

3. What do you do when you **mow** the grass?
   a. cut it
   b. water it
   c. plant it

4. What part of a tree is a **branch**?
   a. the part under the ground
   b. the part that holds the tree up
   c. the parts where leaves grow

5. What does it mean to **earn** money?
   a. to be paid money to do a job
   b. to ask your mother for money
   c. to take money out of your bank

Draw a kite flying high in the sky.

Name _____

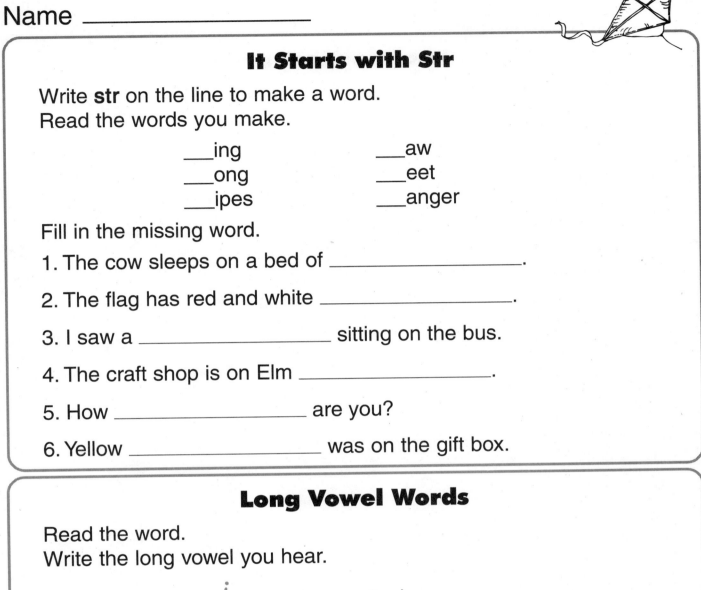

## It Starts with Str

Write **str** on the line to make a word.
Read the words you make.

        ___ing              ___aw

        ___ong             ___eet

        ___ipes           ___anger

Fill in the missing word.

1. The cow sleeps on a bed of _____.

2. The flag has red and white _____.

3. I saw a _____ sitting on the bus.

4. The craft shop is on Elm _____.

5. How _____ are you?

6. Yellow _____ was on the gift box.

## Long Vowel Words

Read the word.
Write the long vowel you hear.

1. Hi _____*i*_____       8. day _____

2. kite _____       9. pie _____

3. stove _____    10. cube _____

4. make _____    11. boat _____

5. go _____       12. tree _____

6. time _____    13. gave _____

7. me _____      14. she _____

Name _____

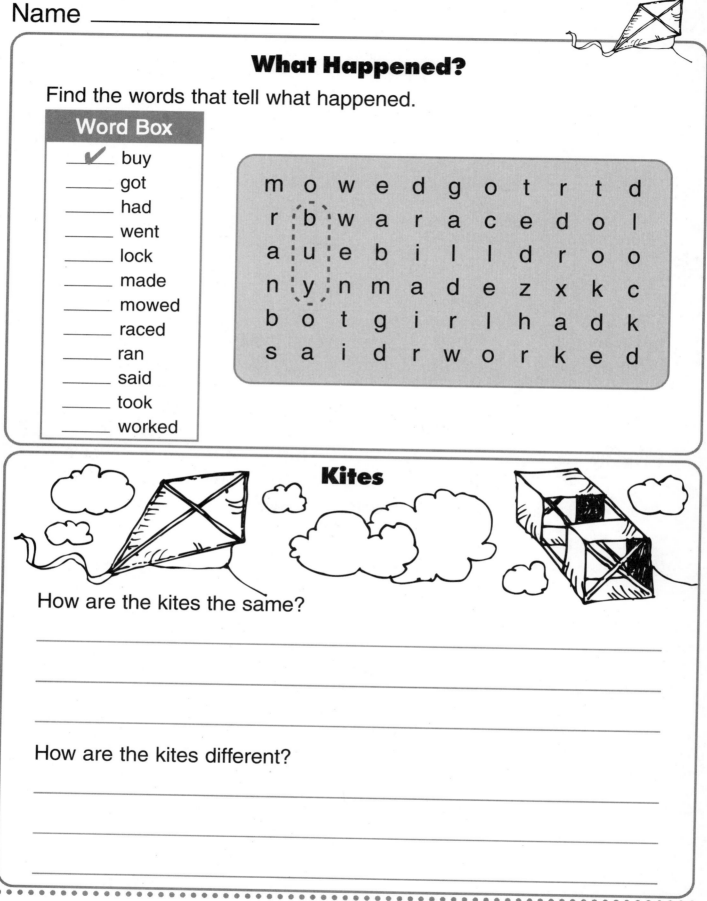

## What Happened?

Find the words that tell what happened.

### Word Box

- ✔ buy
- ____ got
- ____ had
- ____ went
- ____ lock
- ____ made
- ____ mowed
- ____ raced
- ____ ran
- ____ said
- ____ took
- ____ worked

```
m o w e d g o t r t d
r b w a r a c e d o l
a u e b i l l d r o o
n y n m a d e z x k c
b o t g i r l h a d k
s a i d r w o r k e d
```

## Kites

How are the kites the same?

_____

_____

_____

How are the kites different?

_____

_____

_____

   Read and Understand Grade 2 EMC 639

# Popcorn

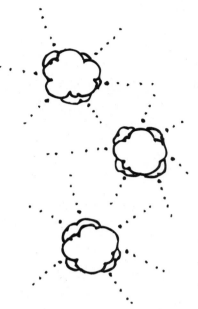

Get out the oil.
Pour some in the pot.
Plop go the kernels.
Now, wait until it's hot!

Pop goes the first kernel.
Pop goes the next.
Then pop, pop...explosion.
There go all the rest!

Think about how popcorn kernels look before they are cooked. How do hard, little, yellow kernels turn into tasty white puffs?

When you cook popcorn the kernels get very hot. Water inside the kernels gets so hot it turns to steam. The hard cover of the kernel keeps the steam in. The steam pushes the hard cover trying to get out. At last the steam pops the cover open. Now you have fluffy puffs of popcorn.

Add a little melted butter and some salt. Snack time!

Read and Understand Grade 2 EMC 639

## Name _____

## **Questions about *Popcorn***

1. How are uncooked popcorn and cooked popcorn different?

   Uncooked popcorn _____

   Cooked popcorn _____

2. What happens to the water in a popcorn kernel when it gets hot?

   _____

   _____

3. How does steam make the kernels pop?

   _____

   _____

4. Why is this kind of corn called popcorn?

   _____

Draw:

| uncooked popcorn | cooked popcorn |
|---|---|
|  |  |

Name _____

## What Happened Next?

Cut out the sentences.
Glue them in order.
Draw pictures in the boxes.
Read the poem.

| | |
|---|---|
| | |
| | |

| | |
|---|---|
| Plop go the kernels.<br>Now, wait until it's hot. | Get out the oil.<br>Pour some in the pot. |
| Pop goes the first kernel.<br>Pop goes the next. | Then pop, pop...explosion.<br>There go all the rest. |

Name _____

# Compound Words

**popcorn** is two small words—**pop** and **corn.**

What small words make these compound words?

1. watermelon      _____ and _____

2. peanut      _____ and _____

3. cowgirl      _____ and _____

4. baseball      _____ and _____

5. buttercup      _____ and _____

6. pancake      _____ and _____

Draw a picture of the compound word.

| | | |
|---|---|---|
| butterfly | cupcake | football |
| cowboy | rainbow | popcorn |

           Read and Understand Grade 2 EMC 639

Name _____

## The Sounds of th

Circle words that say the **th** sound in **the**.
Put an X on words that say the **th** sound in **thing**.

|  |  |  |
|---|---|---|
| then | think | there |
| thin | their | thorn |
| thank | that | thing |

Fill in the missing words.

1. Put it over _____.

2. One cat is fat and one is _____.

3. Did you feel the rose's _____?

4. We ate pizza and _____ we ate ice cream.

5. I _____ it is fun to run.

6. _____ girl ate pizza.

## What Does It Look Like?

Circle words that describe.

|  |  |  |  |
|---|---|---|---|
| hard | little | mouse | jump |
| tasty | white | cold | long |
| run | funny | sad | busy |

Write words that describe.

_____, _____ puppy

_____, _____ ice cream

_____, _____ stick

Name _____

# Popcorn Puzzle

Find the mystery word hiding in the puzzle.

1. break open
2. bubble up and give off steam
3. a sudden bursting
4. the outside of a kernel
5. something to cook in
6. not soft
7. one bit of popcorn

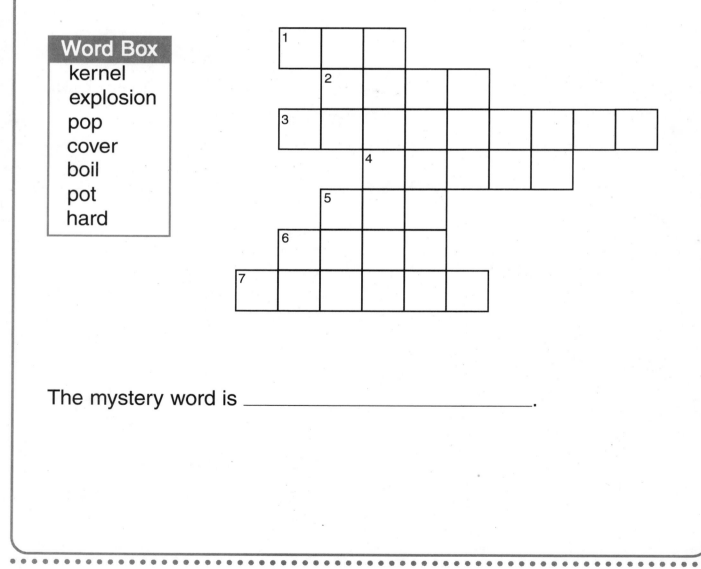

### Word Box
  kernel
  explosion
  pop
  cover
  boil
  pot
  hard

The mystery word is _____.

# Name Day

*Do you have a party on your birthday? If you lived in Greece you would have another party day. It is called Name Day. Read this story to find out what happens on Name Day.*

Church bells were ringing all over Athens. Eleni jumped out of bed and ran to the window to listen. She was very happy. Today was her Name Day.

Eleni ran to the telephone to call her grandmother.

"Happy Name Day, Grandmother," said Eleni. It was her grandmother's Name Day too! They were both named Eleni.

"Eleni, get dressed and come eat your breakfast," called her mother. It is almost time for school."

"Happy Name Day, Eleni," shouted all of her friends at school. Eleni had a surprise for her teacher—a big box of candy! She had more candy to share with her classmates.

As soon as school was out, Eleni ran to Grandmother's house. When she got there, the house was filled with family and friends. Everyone had come to help Eleni and Grandmother celebrate their special day.

"Come here, Eleni," called Grandmother. "I have a gift for you. My mother gave me this when I was just your age. Now it is for you."

"Thank you, Grandmother," whispered Eleni. Her eyes sparkled as she looked at her gift.

"Now, Eleni, it's time for the party," said Grandmother.

There were many good things to eat and then singing and dancing. Name Day was fun for everyone.

Name _____

## Questions About *Name Day*

1. Where did Eleni live?

   _____

2. Why did Eleni call her grandmother before she went to school?

   _____

3. What did she take to her classmates?

   _____

4. Where was the Name Day party?

   _____

5. Why was the Name Day party fun for everyone?

   _____

6. Why did the gift from Grandmother make Eleni so happy?

   _____

7. How is a Name Day party like a birthday party?

   _____

   _____

List two things that made Eleni happy.

1. _____

2. _____

Name _____

# What Happened Next?

Number the sentences in order.

_____ Eleni went to Grandmother's house for a party.

_____ She took candy to school.

_____ She called her Grandmother on the telephone.

_____ Eleni whispered "Thank you."

_1_ Eleni heard the church bells ring.

_____ Grandmother gave Eleni a gift.

Number the pictures in order.

Name _____

## What Does It Mean?

Write the word on the line.

| | |
|---|---|
| whisper | classmates |
| Athens | sparkle |
| celebrate | candy |

1. in the same class _____

2. to speak softly _____

3. a sweet snack _____

4. a city in Greece _____

5. to have a party _____

6. to shine _____

## Who Owns It?

Add 's to these names.
Draw a line to what they own.

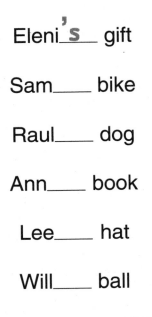

Eleni's gift

Sam___ bike

Raul___ dog

Ann___ book

Lee___ hat

Will___ ball

Read and Understand Grade 2 EMC 639

Name _____

## The Sounds of ed

Read these words. Write them under the letter(s) that stand for the sound you hear at the end of the word.

| ed | d | t |
|---|---|---|
| *wanted* | _____ | _____ |
| _____ | _____ | _____ |
| _____ | _____ | _____ |
| _____ | _____ | _____ |

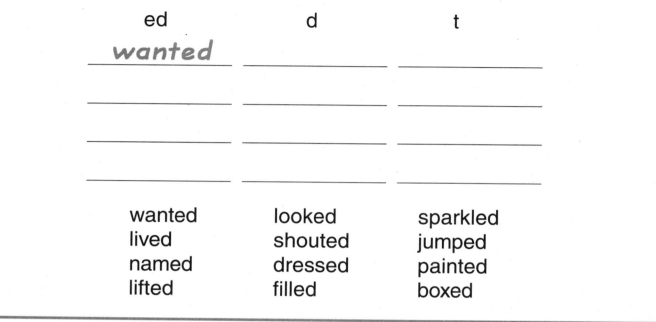

| wanted | looked | sparkled |
|---|---|---|
| lived | shouted | jumped |
| named | dressed | painted |
| lifted | filled | boxed |

## Was or Were?

Fill in **was** or **were**.

He **was** singing.　　(one)
They **were** singing.　(more than one)

1. The bells _____ ringing.

2. She _____ singing a song.

3. Father _____ fixing dinner.

4. His dogs _____ playing with the ball.

5. All the kites _____ up in the sky.

6. The little mouse _____ under the table.

Name _____

# Family Celebrations

Eleni's family celebrates Name Day.
List the days your family celebrates.

_____   _____

_____   _____

_____   _____

This is my family celebrating _____.

We _____

_____

# The Lion and the Mouse

One hot afternoon, a large lion was napping in the shade. A small mouse was looking for a bite of lunch. He ran across the lion's paw. The mouse didn't see danger until it was too late. He was caught in the lion's paw.

"Please don't eat me," begged the little mouse. "Let me go and someday I will repay you."

"How can a little thing like you ever help the King of Beasts?" But the lion let the little mouse go.

A few weeks later, the unhappy lion was trapped in a hunter's net. He roared as he tried to break the strong ropes.

The little mouse heard the lion's loud roars. The mouse thought, "That is the lion that let me go. I must see if I can help him."

The mouse rushed to where the lion was caught. He began to gnaw at the ropes. Before long the lion was free.

"See, I told you I would repay you some day," said the mouse. "Even a tiny mouse can sometimes help the King of Beasts."

Name _____

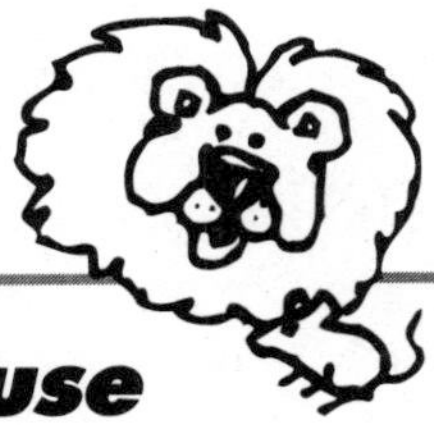

## Questions about *The Lion and the Mouse*

1. Who is this story about?

   _____

2. How did the mouse get caught by the lion?

   _____

3. Where was the lion trapped?

   _____

4. How did the mouse help the lion?

   _____

5. Why do you think the lion let the mouse go?

   _____

6. Why did the mouse help the lion?

   _____

| Draw a lion. | Draw a mouse. |
| --- | --- |
|  |  |

Name _____

# What Happened Next?

Write the sentences in order.

1. _____

2. _____

3. _____

4. _____

> The lion was caught.
> The lion let the mouse go.
> The mouse was caught.
> The mouse let the lion go.

# Lion, Mouse, or Both?

Think about the lion and the mouse.
Write the words that tell ...
    about the lion.
    about the mouse.
    about both of them.

| The lion was... | The mouse was... | They both were... |
| --- | --- | --- |
| _____ | _____ | _____ |
| _____ | _____ | _____ |
| _____ | _____ | _____ |

| large | small | hungry |
| helpful | brave | trapped |
| in danger | unhappy | loud |

Read and Understand Grade 2 EMC 639

Skill: Develop vocabulary.

Name ______________________

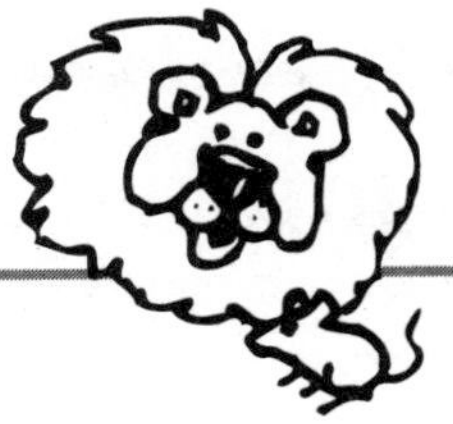

# What Does It Mean?

Write words under the pictures.
You will not use all of the words.

| | | |
|---|---|---|
| lunch | King of Beasts | net |
| trapped | afternoon | roared |
| gnaw | shade | hunter |

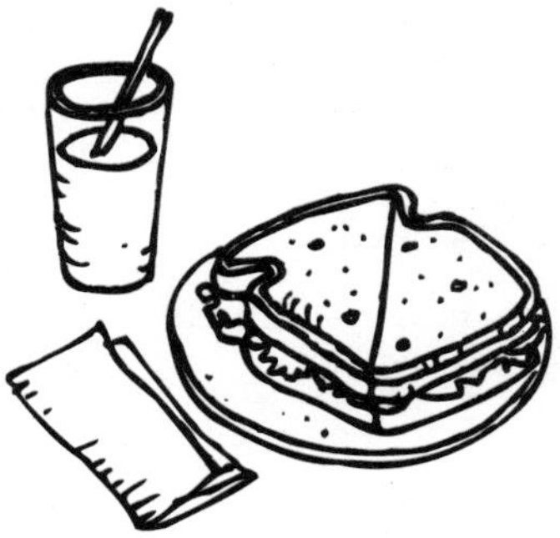
______________

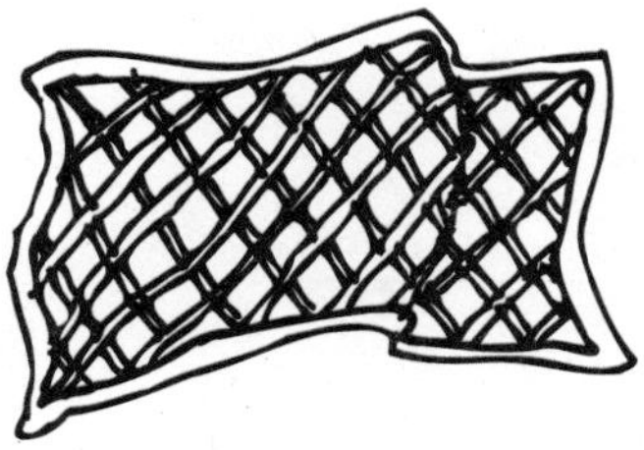
______________

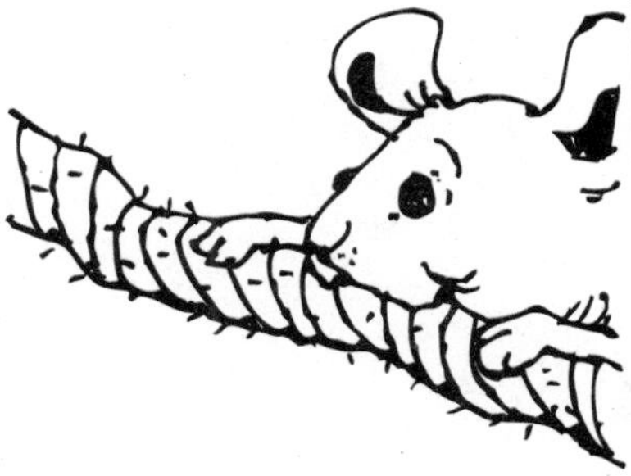
______________

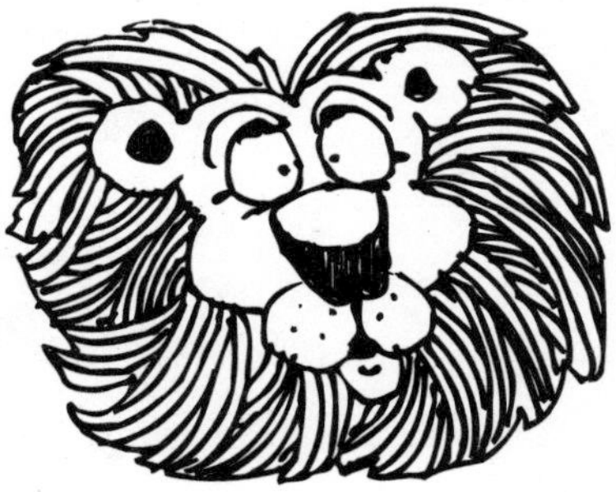
______________

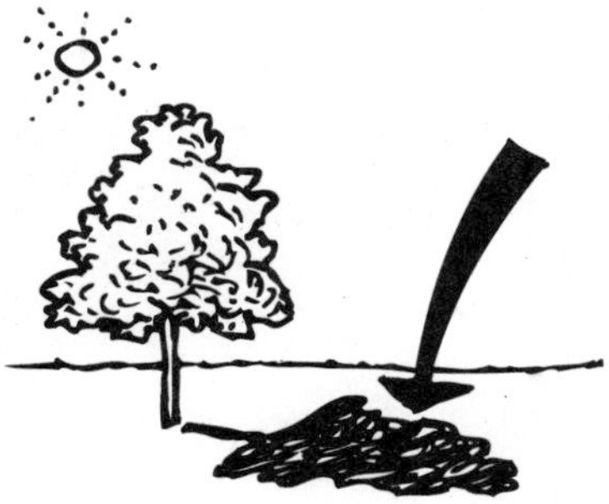
______________

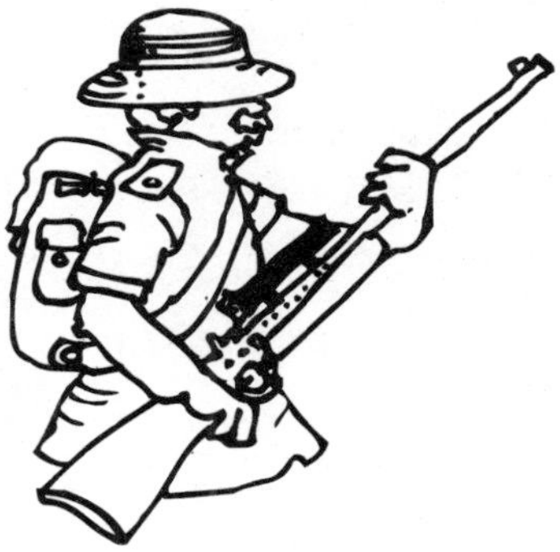
______________

Write sentences with the three of the words.

1. ______________________________________________

2. ______________________________________________

3. ______________________________________________

Name _____

# Word Endings

Add endings to the words.

| | play | play<u>ed</u> | play<u>ing</u> |
|---|---|---|---|
| | | **ed** | **ing** |

1. laugh     _____     _____

2. look     _____     _____

3. roar     _____     _____

Add a letter and endings.

| | drum | drum**m**<u>ed</u> | drum**m**<u>ing</u> |
|---|---|---|---|
| | | **ed** | **ing** |

1. nap     _____     _____

2. beg     _____     _____

3. trap     _____     _____

Fill in the missing word.

1. A lion was _____ in the shade.

2. "Let me go," _____ the mouse.

3. The lion _____ at the mouse.

4. The lion was _____ in a net.

5. The mouse was _____ for the lion.

## Name _____

## Lion and the Mouse Puzzle

**Word Box**
- afternoon
- few
- gnaw
- laugh
- mouse
- roar

**Across**
4. later than noon
5. chew on
6. not a lot

**Down**
1. noise a lion makes
2. a happy sound
3. a small animal

Find the mice hiding in this picture.

I found _____ mice.

# The Best Birthday Ever

"Wake up, Ray," called Mother. "It's time to get up. You don't want to miss the train."

It was Ray's birthday. Today he turned eight years old. He was going with his best friends to visit Mr. Porter's farm.

Ray got dressed and ran downstairs to eat his birthday breakfast.

While he was eating, Connie and Jacob came bouncing in. They were ready to go to the farm.

Jacob grabbed Ray's arm and started to pull him out the door.

"Don't be such a slow poke. It's time to go. I don't want be late. This is the first time I get to ride a train."

The children jumped into Dad's jeep. He drove them to the station and put them on the train. Then he spoke to the conductor.

"Will you see that the children get off at Dayton?" he asked the conductor. "Mr. Porter will be meeting them." The conductor agreed to look after the children.

As the train pulled into Dayton, the children could see Mr. Porter. He helped them off the train and said, "I have a lot planned for Ray's birthday. I think you will all have a good time."

Ray, Connie, and Jacob hopped into the pickup truck. Away they went to the farm.

Mr. Porter was right. Everywhere they looked, there was something fun to do. They painted the hen house. They helped feed the farm animals and tried to milk a cow. They took turns riding a gentle old horse. They had a great day.

"Let's go to the lake," said Mr. Porter. "You can ride in the hay wagon."

"Look at that!" shouted Ray. "There's Mom! And Dad and Mrs. Porter are there too."

What a surprise! A birthday party was set up by the lake. A birthday cake with eight candles, hamburgers, chips, and grape soda—all the things Ray liked best.

It was the best birthday Ray had ever had.

Name _____

## Questions About *The Best Birthday Ever*

1. Where did Ray go on his birthday?

   _____

2. Who went with him?

   _____

3. What five things did the children ride?

   _____  _____  _____

   _____  _____

4. What did Dad ask the train conductor to do?

   _____

   _____

5. Why did Ray think this was his best birthday?

   _____

## Who Said It?

"Wake up, Ray," said _____.

"Don't be such a slow poke," said _____.

"I think you will have a good time," said _____.

"Look at that," shouted _____.

"Mr. Porter will be meeting them," said _____.

Name _____

# What Does It Mean?

**Match:**

best                     don't start yet

wait                    a kind of wall around a yard

slow poke            most good

conductor           someone who is not fast

fence                 in charge of people on a train

Fill in the missing word.

1. Jim painted the backyard _____.

2. The train _____ took my ticket.

3. It is time to go. Don't be such a _____.

4. That was the _____ cake I ever ate.

5. We have to _____ for the train to stop.

# Contractions

Write the contractions for these words.

1. are not _____      4. do not _____

2. I will _____      5. it is _____

3. let us _____      6. can not _____

| it's | let's | aren't |
| I'm | don't | we'll |
| I'll | there's | can't |

# Name _____

## What Came First?

Cut out the sentences.
Paste them in order.

1.

2.

3.

4.

5.

6.

---

"Wake up, Ray. It's time to get up," said Mother.

The children had fun painting the fence.

Dad drove the children to the train.

While Ray was eating breakfast,
Connie and Jacob came in.

A surprise birthday party was set up
by the lake. Ray had a good time.

Ray, Connie, and Jacob rode in the hay wagon.

Name _____

# It Says A

Read these long a words to a friend.

| say | cake | paint |
| play | make | rain |
| day | take | stain |
| way | lake | train |
| stay | wake | wait |

Write the missing letters.

| **ay** | **a - e** | **ai** |

c __ k ____          h ____ ____          r ____ ____ n

cl ____ ____          p ____ ____ nt          sk ____ t ____

**eigh** says **a** too
**eight**

# Name _____

## Happy Birthday _____

Put your name here.

What was the best birthday party you have had?
Tell these things:

Who came to the party?

_____

What did you eat?

_____

What did you do?

_____

_____

Why was it the best party?

_____

_____

Draw you at your best birthday party.

# What's for Lunch?

I have a goat.
What a funny pet.
He'll eat anything
He can get.

crunchy hay
modeling clay
Grandpa's socks
moss on rocks
leaves on trees
beans and peas
labels on cans
greasy pans

Watch him lick.
Watch him munch.
He thinks anything's
A good lunch.

Read and Understand Grade 2 EMC 639

Name _____

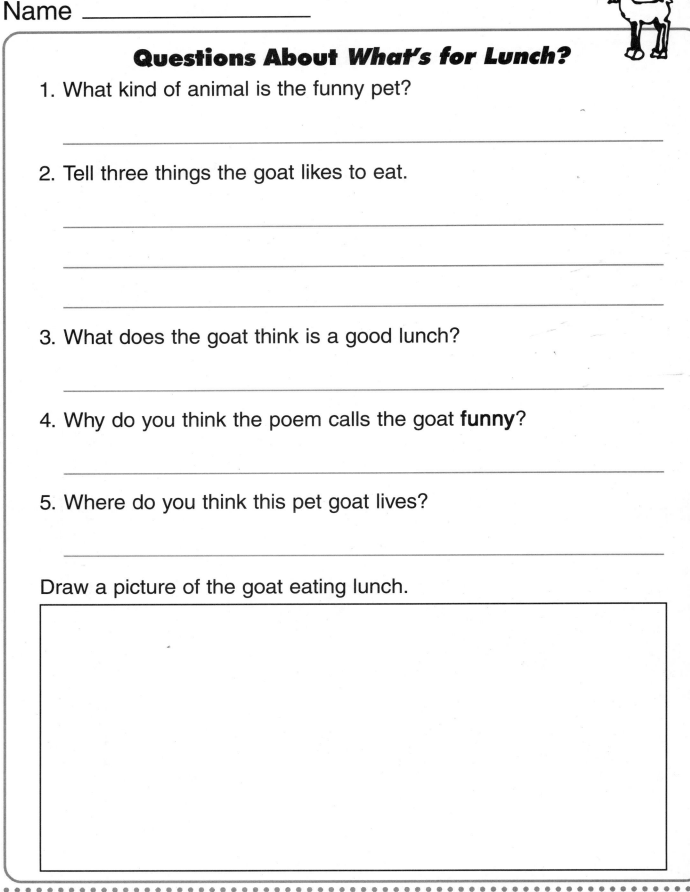

## Questions About *What's for Lunch?*

1. What kind of animal is the funny pet?

   _____

2. Tell three things the goat likes to eat.

   _____

   _____

   _____

3. What does the goat think is a good lunch?

   _____

4. Why do you think the poem calls the goat **funny**?

   _____

5. Where do you think this pet goat lives?

   _____

Draw a picture of the goat eating lunch.

Name _____

## What Rhymes?

Read the poem again.
Write the words that rhyme with these words.

1. pet _____    4. rocks _____

2. hay _____    5. cans _____

3. lunch _____    6. trees _____

You can change the first letter of a word to make a rhyming word.

               **<u>h</u>ay**          **<u>s</u>ay**         **<u>d</u>ay**

1. <u>p</u>et          ____et           ____et

2. <u>l</u>unch       ____unch        ____unch

3. <u>c</u>an          ____an           ____an

4. <u>l</u>ick          ____ick         ____ick

## The Sound of K

All of these words have the sound **k**.
Different letters make the sound in each word.

          c - <u>c</u>an        ck - ro<u>ck</u>        k - <u>k</u>id

Write the letters that say "k" in these words.

sock _____    crunch _____

lick _____    kind _____

kitten _____    candle _____

hike _____    sick _____

Name _____

## What Does It Mean?

Match the word to its meaning.

pet                    the meal we eat in the middle of the day

lunch                  an animal you care for and love

moss                   a paper on a can or jar that tells what
                       is in it

label                  small soft green plants that grow on
                       rocks and trees

munch                  has grease or oil on it

greasy                 to nibble on food

## Contractions

Write the contraction for these words.

1. she will _____    3. I will  _____

2. we will _____     4. they will _____

Write sentences with the contractions.

1. _____

2. _____

3. _____

4. _____

Skills: Categorize items; illustrate information.

Name ______________________

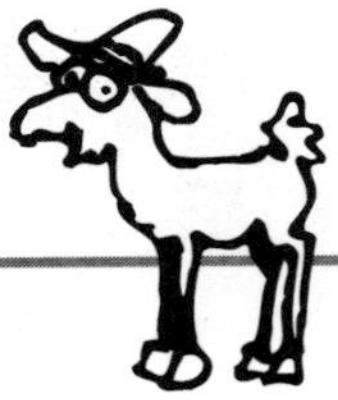

## Lunch Time!

Read the list.
Write the words in the boxes.

| Good for Lunch | Not for Lunch |
|---|---|
| 1. ____________ | 1. ____________ |
| 2. ____________ | 2. ____________ |
| 3. ____________ | 3. ____________ |
| 4. ____________ | 4. ____________ |
| 5. ____________ | 5. ____________ |
| 6. ____________ | 6. ____________ |

| | | |
|---|---|---|
| sandwich | apple | box |
| milk | sock | cookie |
| soup | chicken | mitten |
| bed | grass | mouse |

Draw the lunch you like best.

Name _____

## Real or Make-Believe

*What's For Lunch* is a poem about a make-believe goat that eats anything. Real goats chew and lick many things, but they usually eat plants.

**Circle** the things a real goat would eat.
Put an **X** on things a real goat would not eat.

| | | |
|---|---|---|
| green grass | hay | Grandpa's socks |
| leaves on trees | apples | tin can |
| bedroom slipper | little rocks | carrot sticks |

Connect the dots to see what this make-believe goat is eating.

# Let's Make Cookies

Mark and Art had been playing in the backyard for a long time.

"I want a snack," said Mark. "Let's go get some cookies and milk." Mark loved big, crunchy oatmeal cookies.

The boys looked in the cookie jar, but all the cookies were gone.

"Let's make some," said Mark. After all, he had watched Mom make cookies. It didn't look so hard.

Mark got a box of oatmeal from the cupboard. He got eggs from the refrigerator. Art found the big mixing bowl and a spoon.

Mark broke two eggs into the bowl. He stirred them up just like he had seen his mother do. Art had just started to put in the oatmeal when Mom came in from the garden.

"Just a minute, boys," Mom said. "You need a recipe to make good oatmeal cookies. I'll get it for you. You will need a few more ingredients too."

"What's a recipe?" asked Art. "And what are ingredients?"

"A recipe tells you how to make something," explained Mom. "Ingredients are the things you use to make things to eat.

Mom read the recipe as the boys measured and mixed the dough. When the cookies were in the oven, they all helped clean up the messy kitchen.

"Making cookies is hard work!" said Art. "I think we need a snack." They each had three warm cookies and a big glass of cold milk.

Skills: Recall events in a story; make predictions.

Name ____________________

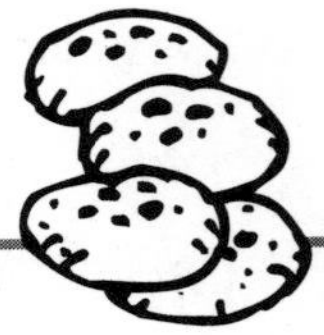

## Questions About *Let's Make Cookies*

1. Where were Mark and Art playing?

______________________________________________

2. Why did the boys start to make cookies?

______________________________________________

3. Tell three ways Mom helped the boys.

______________________________________________

______________________________________________

______________________________________________

4. Why do cooks need recipes?

______________________________________________

______________________________________________

5. What do you think would have happened if Mom had not come home?

______________________________________________

______________________________________________

Name _____

## Cookies

Number the steps in order.

____ Read the recipe.

_1_ The cookie jar is empty.

____ Clean up the kitchen.

____ Mix the cookie dough.

____ Get oatmeal, a bowl, and eggs.

____ Eat cookies and drink milk!

____ Bake the cookies.

## What Did I Say?

Look in the story to see who spoke.
Match each character to what that person said.

"You need a recipe."

Mark        "Making cookies is hard work!"

Mom        "I want a snack."

Art         "Just a minute."

"What are ingredients?"

"Let's make some."

Name _____

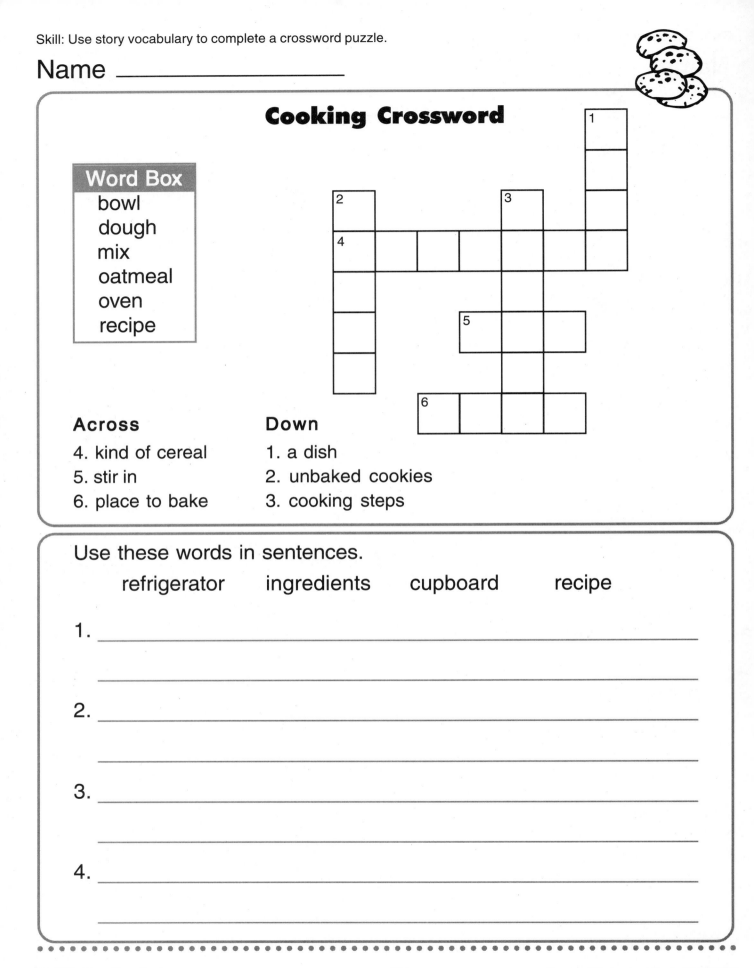

## Cooking Crossword

### Word Box
bowl
dough
mix
oatmeal
oven
recipe

**Across**

4. kind of cereal
5. stir in
6. place to bake

**Down**

1. a dish
2. unbaked cookies
3. cooking steps

---

Use these words in sentences.

refrigerator    ingredients    cupboard    recipe

1. _____

_____

2. _____

_____

3. _____

_____

4. _____

_____

Name _____

## The Sound of ar

All of these words say the **ar** sound.
Read the list to a friend.

| | | |
|---|---|---|
| Mark | jar | hard |
| park | far | card |
| bark | car | part |
| lark | star | start |

Now put in the missing letters.

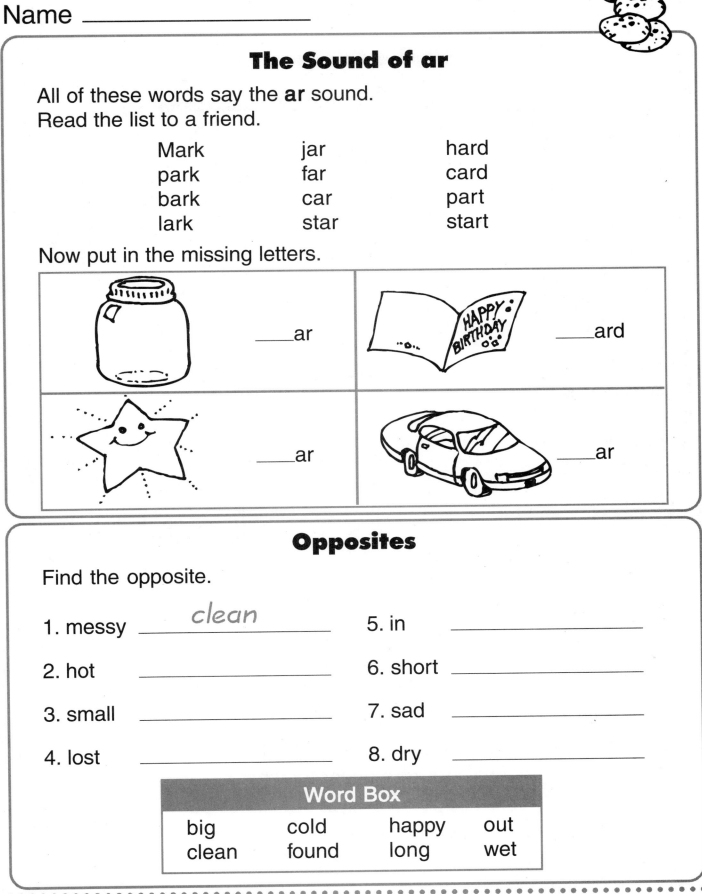

____ar

____ard

____ar

____ar

## Opposites

Find the opposite.

1. messy   *clean* _____

2. hot   _____

3. small   _____

4. lost   _____

5. in   _____

6. short   _____

7. sad   _____

8. dry   _____

| Word Box | | | |
|---|---|---|---|
| big | cold | happy | out |
| clean | found | long | wet |

Name _____

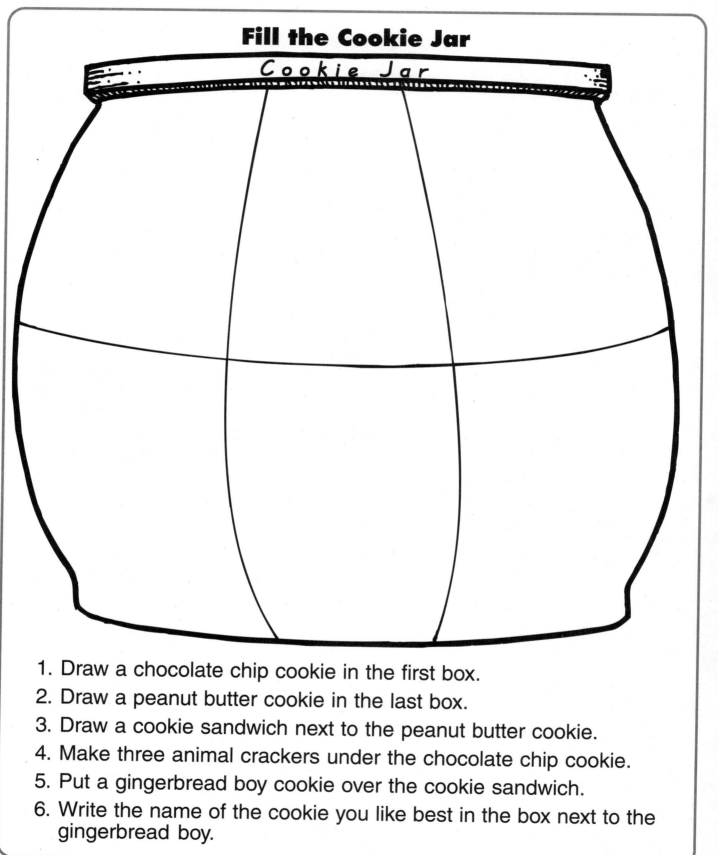

# Fill the Cookie Jar

Cookie Jar

1. Draw a chocolate chip cookie in the first box.
2. Draw a peanut butter cookie in the last box.
3. Draw a cookie sandwich next to the peanut butter cookie.
4. Make three animal crackers under the chocolate chip cookie.
5. Put a gingerbread boy cookie over the cookie sandwich.
6. Write the name of the cookie you like best in the box next to the gingerbread boy.

# The Gingerbread Man

Once upon a time there was a little old woman. She lived in a small cottage with her old husband. They had a tiny dog and a wee cat. One day she made a big gingerbread man for her husband. He loved warm gingerbread. She put it into the oven to bake.

Much to the old woman's surprise the gingerbread man jumped out of the oven. He looked at the old woman and the old man. He looked at the tiny dog and the wee cat. Then, quick as a wink, he ran out the door and down the road.

The old woman and the old man ran after the gingerbread man. They could not catch him. The tiny dog and the wee cat ran after the gingerbread man. They could not catch him. The gingerbread man shouted,

"Run, run, as fast as you can.

You can't catch me,

I'm the gingerbread man."

 Read and Understand Grade 2 EMC 639

The gingerbread man ran on and on. He ran away from a horse and a cow resting in a field. He ran away from a farmer working in the corn field. Horse, cow, and farmer all chased the gingerbread man. Not one of them could catch him. The gingerbread man shouted,

"Run, run, as fast as you can.

You can't catch me,

I'm the gingerbread man."

The gingerbread man came to a wide river. He had to go across the water to get away. As he stood by the river, along came a hungry fox. The fox said,

"I will take you across the river. Just jump up on my back." The gingerbread man did.

The fox went into the river. As he went deeper into the water, the gingerbread man jumped up on the fox's head. Quick as a wink the fox gobbled up the gingerbread man.

"What a tasty snack," said the fox with a smile.

 Read and Understand Grade 2 EMC 639

Skills: Recall information to answer questions. Identify make-believe elements in the story; use creative thinking.

Name _____

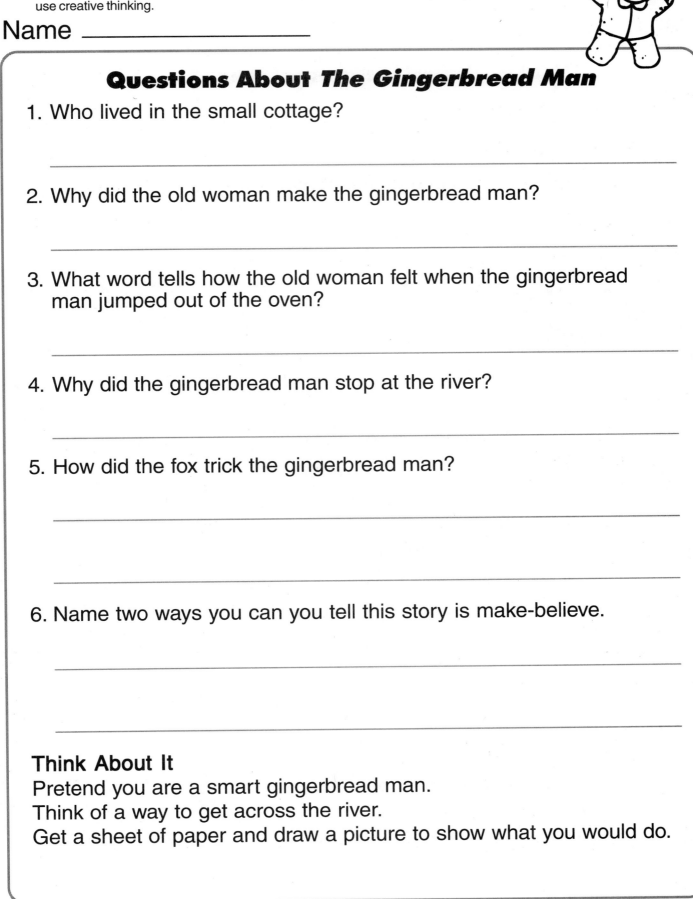

# Questions About *The Gingerbread Man*

1. Who lived in the small cottage?

_____

2. Why did the old woman make the gingerbread man?

_____

3. What word tells how the old woman felt when the gingerbread man jumped out of the oven?

_____

4. Why did the gingerbread man stop at the river?

_____

5. How did the fox trick the gingerbread man?

_____

_____

6. Name two ways you can you tell this story is make-believe.

_____

_____

## Think About It
Pretend you are a smart gingerbread man.
Think of a way to get across the river.
Get a sheet of paper and draw a picture to show what you would do.

Name _____

## What Happened Next?

Number the sentences in order.

____ The gingerbread man ran out of the house.

____ A horse, a cow, and a farmer chased the gingerbread man.

_1_ The old woman made a gingerbread man.

____ The fox went deeper and deeper in the water.

____ The old woman and the old man ran after the gingerbread man.

____ The gingerbread man jumped on the fox's head.

____ The fox gobbled up the gingerbread man.

## People or Animals?

Put these characters in the right place.

old woman          cat and dog
fox                horse and cow
farmer             old man
gingerbread man

**People**

1. _____

2. _____

3. _____

**Animals**

1. _____

2. _____

3. _____

Where does the gingerbread man belong? Why?

_____

_____

Name _____

# What Does It Mean?

Circle the answer.

1. What would you do with a **cottage**?
   a. eat it
   b. wear it
   c. live in it

2. What would you find in a **pasture**?
   a. shop
   b. cow
   c. train

3. What do you do if you **gobble** up something?
   a. play with it
   b. eat it
   c. draw on it

4. What is a **husband**?
   a. a married man
   b. a small boy
   c. a fast runner

5. How fast would **quick as a wink** be?
   a. a minute
   b. a long time
   c. a really short time

6. Find three words in the story that mean **not very big**.

   _____   _____   _____

7. Write a pronoun for each noun.

   cat and dog  _____      old woman  _____

   farmer  _____      gingerbread man  _____

Name _____

# A Word Family—old

Write a letter in front of **old** to make a word family.

_b_old          __old          __old

__old          __old          __old

Write sentences with three of your words.

1. _____

2. _____

3. _____

# The Sounds of G

Read the words.
Write the sound the letter g makes (g or j).

1. gingerbread ___j___          5. giant     _____

2. gobble        ___g___          6. gem      _____

3. gum           _____          7. gate     _____

4. garden        _____          8. giraffe  _____

Name _____

## It Rhymes

Color the words that rhyme.

old—brown     no—red     fox—blue

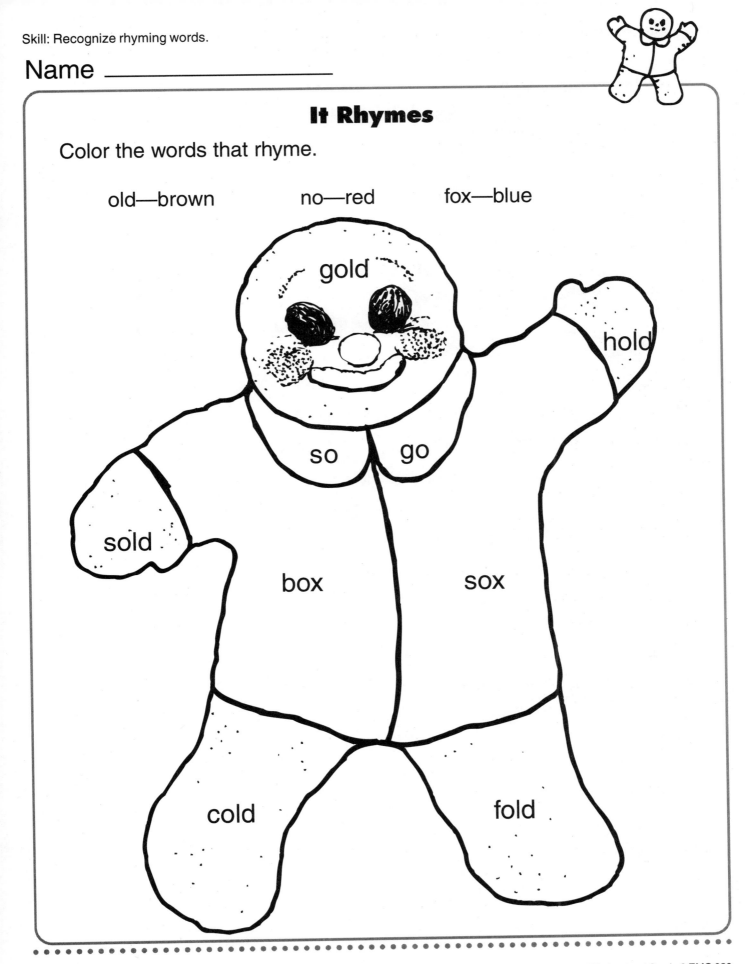

Read and Understand Grade 2 EMC 639

# My Neighbors

Hi, my name is Jamal. That's my house over there. It's the one with the red roof and chimney. My family has lived here all my life. We like living on this block, and we like our neighbors.

Mr. and Mrs. Brown live across the street. Mr. Brown fixes cars and trucks. When my bike was broken, He fixed it for me. Mrs. Brown gives me piano lessons.

Dr. Ramirez lives down the street in the house with fir trees. She was my doctor when I was a baby. She would weigh me and measure me to see how much I was growing. She gave me shots, too.

Aunt Rose lives next door to Mr. and Mrs. Brown in the house with a porch swing. She isn't really my aunt, but she has known me ever since I was born. Aunt Rose is so old she uses a cane when she walks. I like to help her. I take her dog for a walk every day.

Yesterday I went to the store to buy milk and bananas for her. While I was gone she made brownies. We sat on the porch swing and ate brownies and drank milk. Aunt Rose read funny stories from the newspaper. One story was about a man whose hat blew into the gorilla cage at the zoo. The gorilla put on the man's hat and wouldn't give it back.

The best neighbor of all lives next door in the blue house. His name is Gregor. Gregor and I are in the same class at school and play on the same soccer team. Tonight I get to sleep over at Gregor's house. We are going to camp out in the backyard. His dad will put up a tent under the big tree.

Good-bye. I have to pack my bag for tonight.

Name _____

## Questions About *My Neighbors*

1. How long has Jamal lived in the same house?

_____

2. Why does Jamal help Aunt Rose?

_____

3. How does Aunt Rose repay Jamal for his help?

_____

4. Who is the best neighbor? Why?

_____

5. Why does Jamal like living on his block?

_____

## Who Is It?

Give the name of the person.

1. fixes cars and trucks _____

2. is a baby doctor _____

3. bakes brownies _____

4. will set up a tent _____

5. gives piano lessons _____

6. plays soccer with Jamal _____

Name _____

## Jamal's Neighborhood

1. Color the houses.

2. Write Jamal's name on his house.

3. Draw a tent in the backyard of Gregor's house.

4. Put an X on Dr. Ramirez's house.

5. Draw Jamal on Aunt Rose's porch swing.

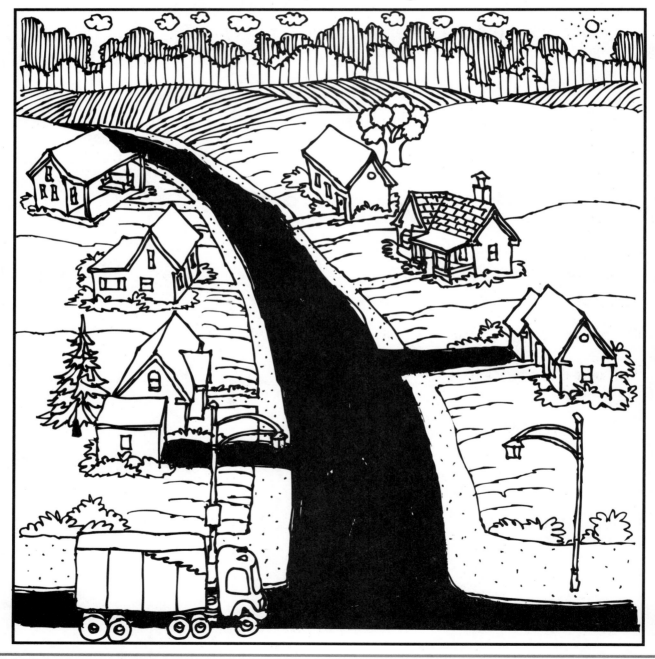

Name _____

## What Does It Mean?

Write the word on the line.

1. people who live on your block _____

2. a tasty snack _____

3. a stick that helps someone walk _____

4. a place in front of the house to sit _____

5. a wild animal _____

6. to spend the night outside _____

7. put things you need in a bag _____

8. flew away _____

**Word Box**

blew
brownies
camp out
cane
gorilla
neighbors
pack
porch

Draw a picture of Jamal and Gregor camping out in the backyard.

Name _____

## Eigh says A

Fill in the missing letters **eigh**.

_____t          w_____          n_____bor

Read the words.
Write a sentence with each word.

1. _____

2. _____

3. _____

## Words That Sound the Same

Read the words to a friend.

| | | | |
|---|---|---|---|
| blew | blue | see | sea |
| red | read | way | weigh |
| buy | by | ate | eight |

Fill in the missing word.

1. The man's hat _____ into the gorilla's cage.

2. Aunt Rose _____ the newspaper.

3. Jamal went to _____ milk and bananas.

4. How much do you _____?

5. I _____ brownies and milk.

6. Gregor lives in a _____ house.

7. Do you know the _____ to the store?

8. My dog had _____ puppies.

     Read and Understand Grade 2 EMC 639

Name _____

## My Neighborhood

Draw a picture of your neighborhood.

Write about the people who live in your neighborhood.

_____

_____

_____

_____

_____

_____

# Frogs

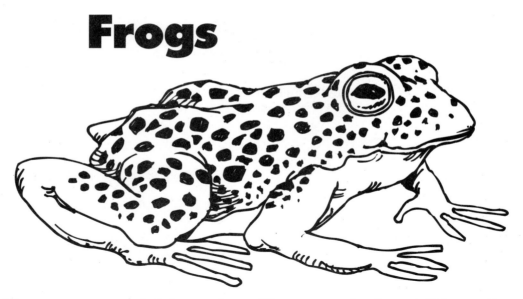

Frogs are amphibians (am-**fib**-ee-uns). Amphibians live in wet places. Some frogs live on land near water. Some frogs live in water all the time. Some frogs live in trees. A few kinds of frogs dig burrows underground.

A frog has smooth, moist skin. It has a big head, no neck, and a short, round body. Big eyes sit on top of the frog's head. The frog can peek out of the water without sticking its head above the water. This helps keep the frog safe from hungry enemies.

A toad is one kind of frog. It has bumpy skin that is not as moist as the skin of other frogs.

A frog has four legs. Its back legs are big and strong. This makes the frog a good jumper. The front legs on a frog are smaller than the back legs. The frog rests its front feet on the ground when it sits. Sometimes it uses the front feet like hands to push food into its mouth.

Frogs that live by ponds and streams have webbed feet for swimming. Tree frogs have sticky toes for climbing trees. Frogs that dig burrows have pointed toes for digging.

A frog doesn't drink like you do. Its skin lets the water in, so frogs must live where they can get into water.

A hungry frog sits very still. When an insect gets close, the frog's sticky tongue zips out and grabs it for dinner. A frog eats small animals like snails and worms, too.

A frog starts as a tadpole hatched from a jelly-like egg. The tadpole has no legs, a long tail, and gills like a fish.

The tadpole moves its tail from side to side to swim. It swims in the water looking for food. It eats little plants called algae (**al**- jee).

The tadpole's back legs grow first. Then its front legs grow. As the legs grow, the tail gets shorter. Lungs begin to grow, too. Soon the tadpole will look like a frog. The frog will jump out of the water to live on land, but it will stay by the water.

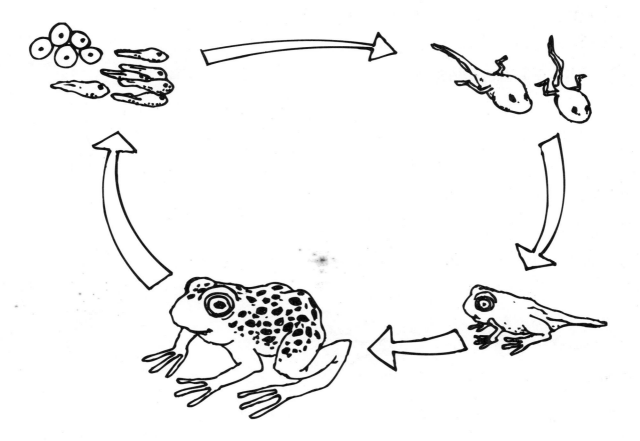

    Read and Understand Grade 2 EMC 639

Name _____

## Questions About *Frogs*

1. What do frogs' eggs look like?

_____

2. How do amphibians drink water?

_____

3. How do frogs catch dinner?

_____

4. What are webbed feet used for?

_____

5. What do tadpoles use to get air?

_____

6. What do tadpoles eat?

_____

7. How is a tree frog different from a pond frog?

_____

What am I?

_____        _____        _____

Name _____

# A Frog Is Born

Cut out the sentences and paste them in order.
Draw a picture for each sentence.

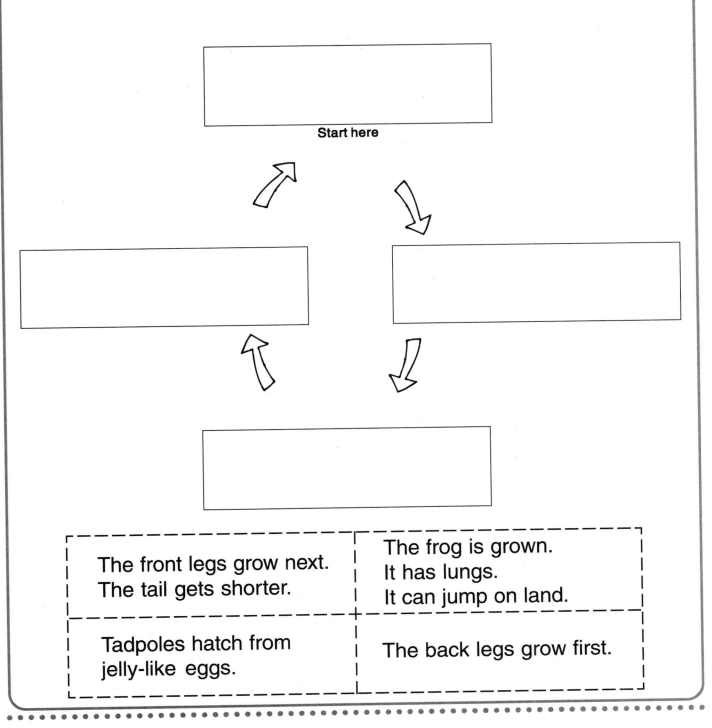

Start here

| The front legs grow next. The tail gets shorter. | The frog is grown. It has lungs. It can jump on land. |
|---|---|
| Tadpoles hatch from jelly-like eggs. | The back legs grow first. |

Read and Understand Grade 2 EMC 639

Name _____

# What Does It Mean?

Fill in the blanks.

1. A _____ has bumpy skin.

2. A _____ has smooth skin.

3. Frogs and toads are _____.

4. Tadpoles use _____ to get air.

5. Frogs have _____ skin.

6. Tadpoles eat _____.

7. Some toads live in _____ underground.

algae            gills
amphibians       moist
burrows          toad
frog

Read and color.

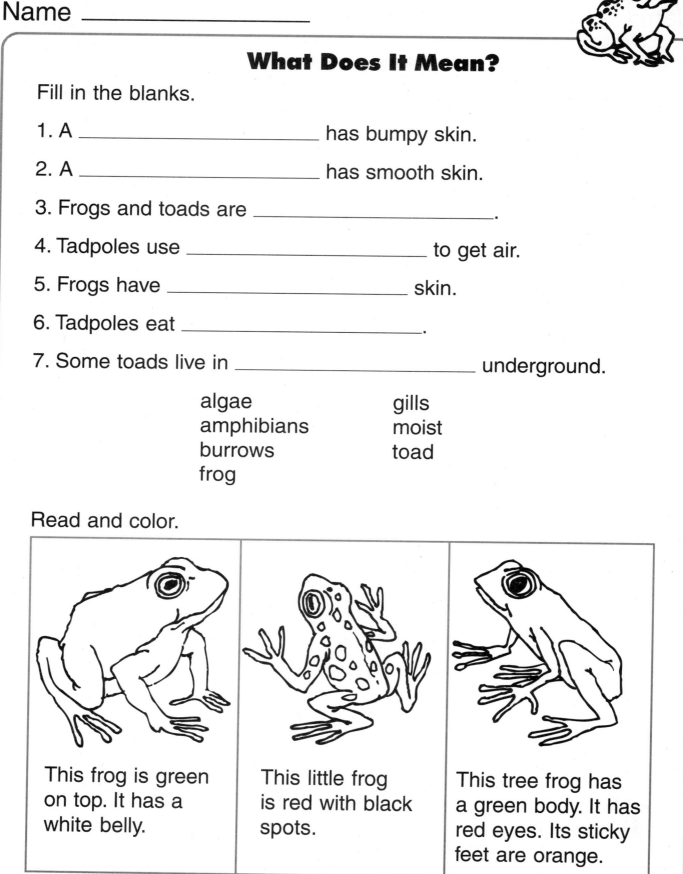

This frog is green on top. It has a white belly.

This little frog is red with black spots.

This tree frog has a green body. It has red eyes. Its sticky feet are orange.

Read and Understand Grade 2 EMC 639

Name _____

# oi—oy

The letters **oi** and **oy** make the same sound.

    **oy**—at the end of a word: b**oy**

    **oi**—at the beginning or in the middle: **oi**l m**oi**st

Put the missing letters in these words.

    1. b____l      3. ____l      5. s____l

    2. t____      4. R____      6. m____st

Fill in the missing word.

1. The hot water began to _____.

2. Carlos has a _____ dinosaur.

3. The frog had _____ skin.

4. Dad put _____ in the car.

5. His name is _____.

6. Father planted the seeds in _____.

# Words That Mean the Same

A frog can **jump**.     A frog can **hop**.

Write words that mean the same.

1. little _____      5. big _____

2. grin _____      6. yell _____

3. wet _____      7. happy _____

4. fast _____      8. pokey _____

    small     moist     large     smile

    glad      slow     shout     quick

Name _____

## Is It a Frog?

Circle the answer.

|     |                       |       |    |
| --- | --------------------- | ----- | -- |
| 1.  | strong back legs      | (yes) | no |
| 2.  | moist skin            | yes   | no |
| 3.  | scales                | yes   | no |
| 4.  | live by water         | yes   | no |
| 5.  | sticky tongue         | yes   | no |
| 6.  | jelly-like eggs       | yes   | no |
| 7.  | no legs               | yes   | no |
| 8.  | starts as a tadpole   | yes   | no |
| 9.  | no neck               | yes   | no |
| 10. | slithers along        | yes   | no |
| 11. | hops along            | yes   | no |

What Am I?

Look at your **no** answers.
Draw an animal with those characteristics.

# It's Raining

Drip, drop. Drip, drop. Drip, drop. Splash! Rain falls down, wetting the land and making puddles. But how does water get up in the sky? How does it fall down on the earth? Read about how it happens.

The hot sun warms the earth. The heat changes water into water vapor. Water vapor is always in the air, but it is invisible.

You can see water vapor change to water drops when you breathe on a cold day. There is water vapor in the warm air you breathe out. When that water vapor hits the cold air outside, it turns into little drops. It looks like a little cloud is coming out of your mouth. You can also see water vapor change to water drops when steam comes out of a tea kettle.

Warm air carries the water vapor up in the sky. When the warm air meets cold air high in the sky, the water vapor turns into little drops of water.

When millions of little drops come together they make a cloud. As the little drops get together, they make bigger drops. When the drops get too big and too heavy, they fall down to the earth as rain.

This is called the water cycle.

 Read and Understand Grade 2 EMC 639

Name _____

# Questions About *It's Raining*

1. What does the heat of the sun do to water?

   _____

2. How does water vapor get up into the sky?

   _____

3. What is a cloud?

   _____

4. What makes the water in a cloud fall as rain?

   _____

   _____

What is happening in this picture?

_____

_____

_____

_____

_____

Name _____

# The Water Cycle

Cut out the sentences.
Paste them in order.

### The heat of the sun warms the earth.

| |
|---|
| |
| |
| |
| |
| |
| |

### The cycle starts again.

- - - - - - - - - - - - - - - - - - - - - - - - - - - - - - -

The water vapor goes up into the sky.

The heat changes water into water vapor.

The water drops get big and heavy.

It begins to rain.

The water drops become a cloud.

The water vapor becomes drops of water.

Read and Understand Grade 2 EMC 639

Name _____

# What Does It Mean?

Draw a line from the word to its meaning.

puddle         can't be seen

invisible       our planet

Earth         a pool of water

cloud         a lot of drops of water together in the sky

rain          weighs a lot

heavy        drops of water falling from the sky

breathe      take air in and out of your lungs

# Opposites

Write the opposites for these words.

dry      _____

small   _____

up       _____

low      _____

large    _____

light    _____

hot      _____

apart   _____

## Word Box

high
little
wet
down
heavy
big
together
cold

Read and Understand Grade 2 EMC 639

Name _____

# It Says ow

Fill in the missing letters—**ow** or **ou**.

| cl____d | c____ | fr____n |
|---|---|---|
| h____se | m____th | cl____n |

Circle the missing word.

1. A big _____ came to the sale.          croud     crowd

2. Let's ride our bikes _____ the hill.          doun     down

3. _____! That hurt.          Ouch     Owch

4. The baby goats ran _____ the haystack.          around     arownd

# Er—Or

Circle the letters that say **/er/**.

color          butterfly
water          vapor
storyteller    flavor
doctor         singer

Write sentences with two of the words.

1. _____

2. _____

Name _____

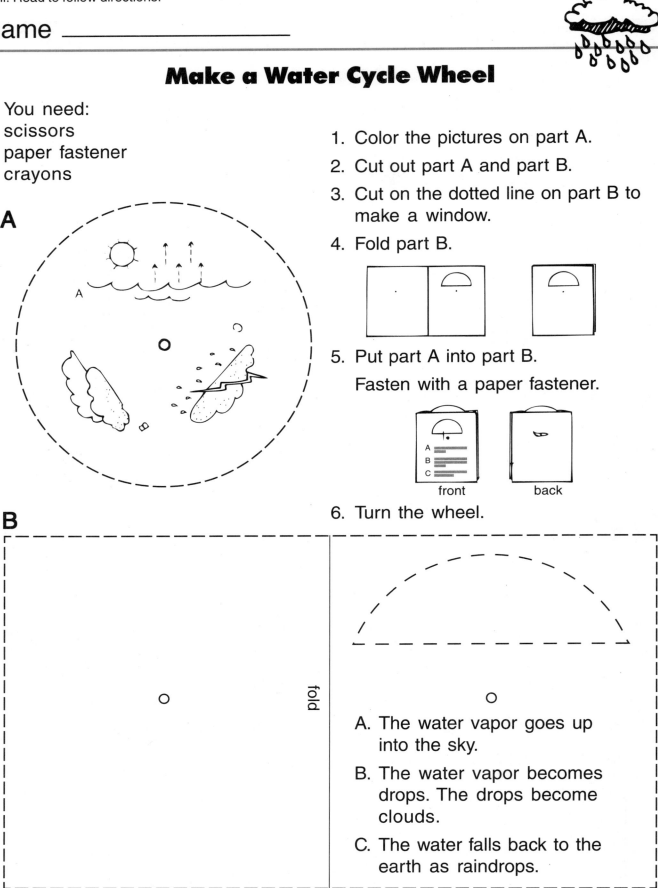

# Make a Water Cycle Wheel

You need:
scissors
paper fastener
crayons

**A**

1. Color the pictures on part A.
2. Cut out part A and part B.
3. Cut on the dotted line on part B to make a window.
4. Fold part B.

5. Put part A into part B.

   Fasten with a paper fastener.

   front          back

6. Turn the wheel.

**B**

fold

A. The water vapor goes up into the sky.

B. The water vapor becomes drops. The drops become clouds.

C. The water falls back to the earth as raindrops.

# Ducks Don't Get Wet

A duck is waterproof.
Water rolls off his back.
Because oil and water don't mix
And that's a proven fact.

Preening every day
In damp or sunny weather,
He spreads oil with his bill
Over each lovely feather.

When he dives under water
Looking for food to eat,
His oily feathers keep him dry
From his head down to his feet.

A duck is waterproof.
Water rolls off his back
Because oil and water don't mix
And that's a proven fact.

Name _____

## Questions About *Ducks Don't Get Wet*

1. Why does a duck need oily feathers?

   _____

   _____

2. Where does a duck find food?

   _____

3. How does a duck spread oil over its feathers?

   _____

4. What does the poem tell you will not mix together?

   _____

5. What word in this poem rhymes with:

   feather _____

   feet _____

6. Where could you go to see a duck in water?

   _____

   _____

Skill: Record information.

Name ____________________

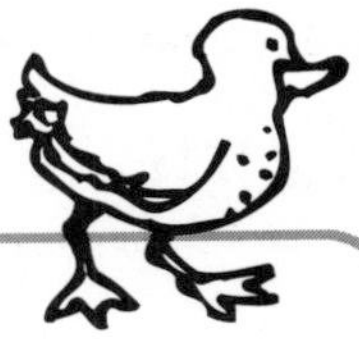

## A Duck Doesn't Get Wet

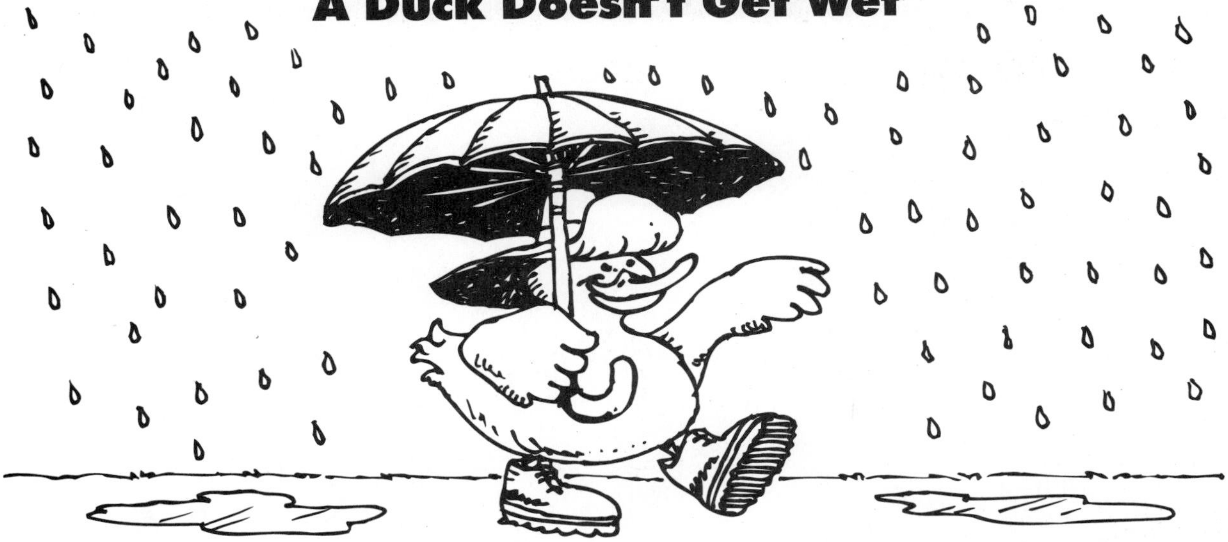

Tell how a duck keeps its feathers dry when it is in the water.

Name _____

# What Does It Mean?

Color in the circle to show what the word means.

1. In the story **preen** means to:
   ○ jump up and down
   ○ dive in the water
   ○ rub oil on feathers

2. A **bird** is animal that is covered in:
   ○ scales
   ○ feathers
   ○ hair

3. If something is **oily**:
   ○ it is covered in oil
   ○ it eats oil
   ○ it cooks with oil

4. **Waterproof** means:
   ○ there is water in it
   ○ water rolls off it
   ○ water makes it wet

5. When you are **damp**:
   ○ you are a little wet
   ○ you need to sleep
   ○ you want a snack

6. What word is the opposite of **sunny**?
   ○ funny
   ○ windy
   ○ cloudy

7. What is another way to say **do not**?
   ○ dont
   ○ donn't
   ○ don't

Read and Understand Grade 2 EMC 639

Name _____

## What Does It Say?

The letters **ee** and **ea** say the sound of long **e**.
Draw these pictures.

| | | |
|---|---|---|
| bee | peas | beads |
| tree | seeds | knee |
| ice cream | tea | peach |

Circle the missing word.

1. Lee likes to eat ice _____.                      cream   creem

2. The bumble _____ buzzed.                         bea     bee

3. Grandmother made me a cup of _____.             tea     tee

4. Will you help me plant the _____?               seads   seeds

5. I fell and bumped my _____.                     knea    knee

6. Did you water the _____ plants in the garden?  pea     pee

 Read and Understand Grade 2 EMC 639

Name _____

## **Water and Oil**

Do this experiment:

1. Cut out the duck.
2. Rub oil on part of the duck.
3. Put a few drops of water on the oily part.
4. Put a few drops of water on the part with no oil.

What did you see?

# Pests in the Vegetable Patch

Aunt Gertie planted a big garden. She watered it. She weeded it. And she waited as it grew. One sunny day, the vegetables were ready to harvest. Aunt Gertie took her basket and headed for the vegetable patch to pick something for lunch.

She walked through the garden gate singing a happy song. Suddenly, her eyes popped open. Her mouth flew open too. This is what she saw...

A bunny munching the cabbage.

A mouse nibbling on peas.

A crow snacking on corn.

A gopher eating lettuce—roots, leaves, and all.

The garden was full of pesky critters eating her vegetables.

"Shoo," shouted Aunt Gertie. "I grew these vegetables for me. I need them for soup. I need them for salad." The animals scurried away. Aunt Gertie picked what she needed for lunch.

 Read and Understand Grade 2 EMC 639

"It's time to fix dinner," thought Aunt Gertie. She picked up her basket and walked to the vegetable patch. This is what she saw.

A bunny munching the cabbage.
A mouse nibbling on peas.
A crow snacking on corn.
A gopher eating lettuce—roots, leaves, and all.
Those pesky critters were back again.

"Shoo," shouted Aunt Gertie. "How am I going to keep you out of my garden?" Every day the pesky critters were in the vegetable patch. Every day Aunt Gertie tried to shoo them away.

The next spring Aunt Gertie planted two gardens. She planted one garden for the pesky critters. Then she planted a garden for herself—with all the plants in wire baskets.

"That should keep those pesky critters out of my garden!" Aunt Gertie declared.

Name _____

## Questions About *Pests in the Vegetable Patch*

1. How did Aunt Gertie take care of her garden?

   _____

2. Why did Aunt Gertie plant a garden?

   _____

3. What did she look like when she saw the animals eating her vegetables?

   _____

   _____

4. Name the pesky critters and tell what they ate.

   a. _____  _____     c. _____  _____

   b. _____  _____     d. _____  _____

5. What did Aunt Gertie do to protect her new spring garden?

   _____

6. Will the wire baskets keep out the critters? Why?

   _____

   _____

How did Aunt Gertie feel?
Put an **X** when she felt happy.
Put a ✔ when she was not happy.

____ planted her garden          ____ watched her garden grow
____ shouted "shoo"              ____ saw critters eating her
____ her mouth flew open              vegetables
____ was singing a song          ____ ate the vegetables in soup

# Name _____

## What Happened Next?

Draw a picture to show what happened next.

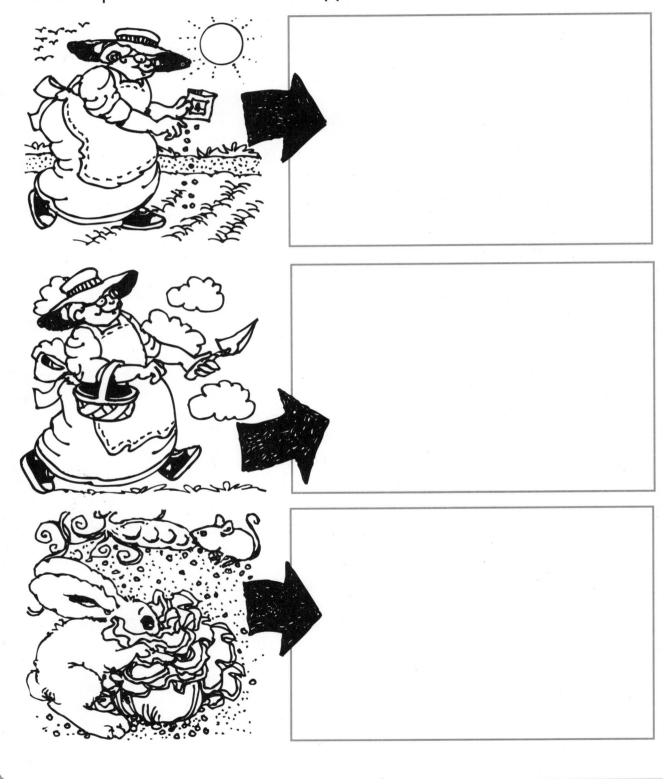

Name _____

## What Does It Mean?

What do these words mean in the story?

| | |
|---|---|
| harvest | garden |
| pesky | munch |
| shoo | vegetable patch |
| weeded | critters |

1. a kind of garden ___*vegetable patch*___

2. a funny name for animals _____

3. a place to grow plants like vegetables _____

4. pick the ripe vegetables _____

5. a noise that says "go away" _____

6. pulled out unwanted plants _____

7. bothersome _____

8. chew _____

## In the Garden

Draw these things that were in the garden.

| | | |
|---|---|---|
| bunny | peas | mouse |
| crow | lettuce | corn |

Read and Understand Grade 2 EMC 639

Name _____

## Ou—Ow

Read the words.
Circle the letters that say **ow**.

| | | | |
|---|---|---|---|
| how | out | flour | cow |
| clown | shout | house | frown |
| mouth | flower | town | mouse |

Fill in the blanks.

1. _____ do you make pancakes?

2. Don't let the dog lick you on your _____.

3. That funny _____ made me happy.

4. We get milk from a _____.

5. Take _____ the trash.

6. You will wake the baby if you _____ in the house.

## Add ly

Change these words by adding **ly** at the end.
Use the new words in sentences.

quick_____      slow_____      sudden_____

1. _____

2. _____

3. _____

Name _____

# Aunt Gertie

Write about a time in the story when Aunt Gertie felt this way.

1. Aunt Gertie was happy _____

_____

_____ .

2. Aunt Gertie was angry _____

_____

_____ .

3. Aunt Gertie was surprised _____

_____

_____ .

4. Aunt Gertie was smart _____

_____

_____ .

5. Aunt Gertie was kind _____

_____

_____ .

# Penguins

Most penguins live in a land of snow and ice. They have feathers, wings, and a beak like other birds. But they are different in two important ways.

Penguins cannot fly. A penguin body is too heavy. Its wings are small, flat, and stiff.

The feet of a penguin are made for swimming, not walking. Penguins look funny as they waddle across land. If they want to move quickly on land, they flop down on their bellies and slide. In the water they use their webbed feet to help them swim.

The way penguins use their wings is different, too. They use their flat, stiff wings as flippers to help them swim swiftly through the cold water. They swim as well as the fish, seals, and whales.

When a penguin is hungry, it dives into the ocean and hunts for food. Penguins eat shrimplike animals called krill. They also eat squid and fish.

Penguins lay eggs like all birds. Some kinds of penguins make a nest of pebbles. One kind holds the egg on its feet. The penguin covers the egg with a flap of skin to keep it warm.

Penguin chicks are covered with fluffy feathers when they hatch. Both the mother and father penguin feed the baby. When the chick grows adult feathers, it will go to the ocean to get its own food.

Read and Understand Grade 2 EMC 639

Name _____

## Questions About *Penguins*

1. Why can't a penguin fly?

_____

2. How can a penguin swim so well?

_____

3. Where does a penguin find its food?

_____

4. What do penguins eat?

_____

5. Give two ways a penguin might keep its egg warm.

   a. _____

   b. _____

6. How do penguin chicks look different than their parents?

   a. A chick is _____

   b. Penguin parents are _____

## Find the Birds

p e n g u i n g p
j e a g l e w u e
a d u c k h r l a
y f i n c h e l c
c h i c k e n z o
m p e l i c a n c
o w l x l a r k k

___ chicken       ___ lark
___ duck          ___ owl
___ eagle         ___ peacock
___ finch         ___ pelican
___ gull          ___ penguin
___ jay           ___ wren

Read and Understand Grade 2 EMC 639

Name _____

# What Does it Mean?

Read the story to find the missing words.

1. All birds are covered in _____.

2. A baby penguin is called a _____.

3. _____ are shrimplike animals eaten by penguins.

4. Penguins _____ when they walk across land.

5. Penguins slide across the ice on their _____.

6. Penguins have _____ feet for swimming.

# Penguin Crossword Puzzle

**Word Box**
- beak
- eggs
- feathers
- flippers
- hatch
- krill
- nest
- penguin
- swift
- swim

**Across**

2. these cover birds
3. to move in the water
5. a bird that cannot fly
8. a shrimplike animal
9. quick

**Down**

1. a bird's bill
2. penguins use their wings as
4. a bird hatches from this
6. home for some bird eggs
7. come out of an egg

Read and Understand Grade 2 EMC 639

Name _____

## A Penguin Is Born

Cut out the pictures at the bottom of the page.
Paste them in order.

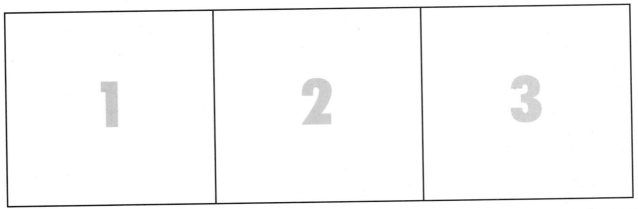

How do penguin parents take care of the egg?

_____

_____

_____

How do they take care of the chick after the egg hatches?

_____

_____

_____

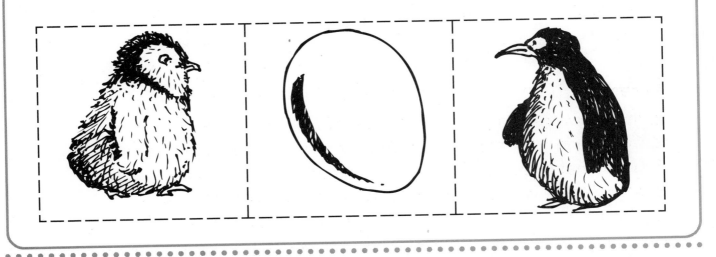

Read and Understand Grade 2 EMC 639

Name _____

# Add an Ending

Add the endings to these words.

|         | er | ly |
|---------|------|------|
| quick   | _____ | _____ |
| soft    | _____ | _____ |
| swift   | _____ | _____ |
| slow    | _____ | _____ |
| quiet   | _____ | _____ |

Fill in the missing ending.

1. Tom sang loud<u>er</u> than Mark did.

2. Kyle spoke soft____ so he wouldn't wake the baby.

3. The penguin swam swift____ in the water.

4. A rabbit is quick____ than a snail.

5. How slow____ can you drink your milk?

6. You may play quiet____ until bedtime.

Name _____

# Penguins and Robins Are Birds

Fill in the chart to compare a penguin and a robin.

|  | penguin | robin |
|---|---|---|
| can fly |  |  |
| cannot fly |  |  |
| swims |  |  |
| has feathers |  |  |
| mother lays eggs |  |  |
| has webbed feet |  |  |
| have beaks |  |  |
| eats worms |  |  |
| eats krill |  |  |
| feed baby chicks |  |  |
| one egg |  |  |
| many eggs |  |  |
| have wings |  |  |
| chirps a song |  |  |

# The Chimpanzee's Friend

What would your mother say if you took worms to bed? What if you hid in a chicken house for hours? A little girl growing up in England did these things. Her name was Jane Goodall.

Jane always loved animals. When she was a baby, she slept with a toy chimpanzee. When she was two years old, she hid earthworms under her pillow. She wanted to see what they did at night. When she was four years old, she hid in a chicken house and stayed there until she saw a chicken lay an egg.

When Jane grew up she went to Africa. She wanted to learn more about animals. She began watching chimpanzees on a reserve in Tanzania. She waited and watched until the chimps were not afraid of her.

Jane watched the chimps for many years. She saw baby chimps grow up and start families of their own. She knew each chimp when she saw it and even gave the chimps names.

She learned how chimpanzees behave. She learned what they eat and how they take care of their babies. She saw how they get along with other chimpanzees. Her notes about what she saw have helped other scientists understand how animals behave.

Today Jane Goodall travels around the world talking to people about why we need to protect animals.

Skills: Read for information; answer questions.

Name ____________________

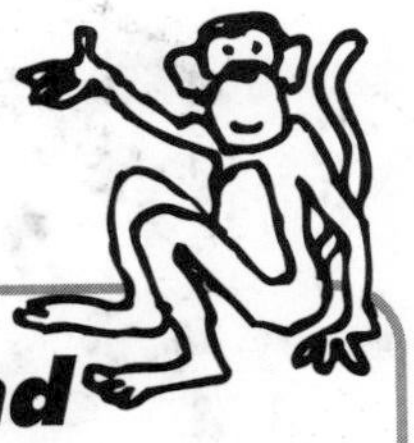

## Questions About *The Chimpanzee's Friend*

1. Where did Jane Goodall grow up?

______________________________

2. Why did she put earthworms under her pillow?

______________________________

3. How did she learn about hens laying eggs?

______________________________

4. Where did she go in Africa?

______________________________

5. What animal did she study?

______________________________

6. How did she learn about the animals?

______________________________

7. What is Jane Goodall doing now?

______________________________

Have you ever watched an animal? yes no

What animal did you watch? ______________________________

What did you see? ______________________________

______________________________

______________________________

______________________________

Name _____

## What Happened Next?

Cut out the sentences.
Paste them in order.

1. [                                        ]

2. [                                        ]

3. [                                        ]

4. [                                        ]

5. [                                        ]

6. [                                        ]

---

She slept with a toy chimp when she was a baby.

She watched chimpanzees in Africa.

She hid earthworms under her pillow.

Jane Goodall was born in England.

She talks about why we need to protect animals.

She watched a hen lay an egg.

Name _____

# What Does It Mean?

Write the letter of each answer.

1. What did **watch** mean in the story?

2. Where is **Tanzania**?

3. What do you do if you take **notes**?

4. What does **travel** mean?

5. What did **behave** mean in the story?

6. What is an animal **reserve**?

A. to look at something
B. write down what you see
C. to act or do things

D. a safe place for animals
E. to go from place to place
F. in Africa

Draw:

| | |
|---|---|
| pillow | earthworm |
| chimpanzee | hen and egg |

Read and Understand Grade 2 EMC 639

Name _____

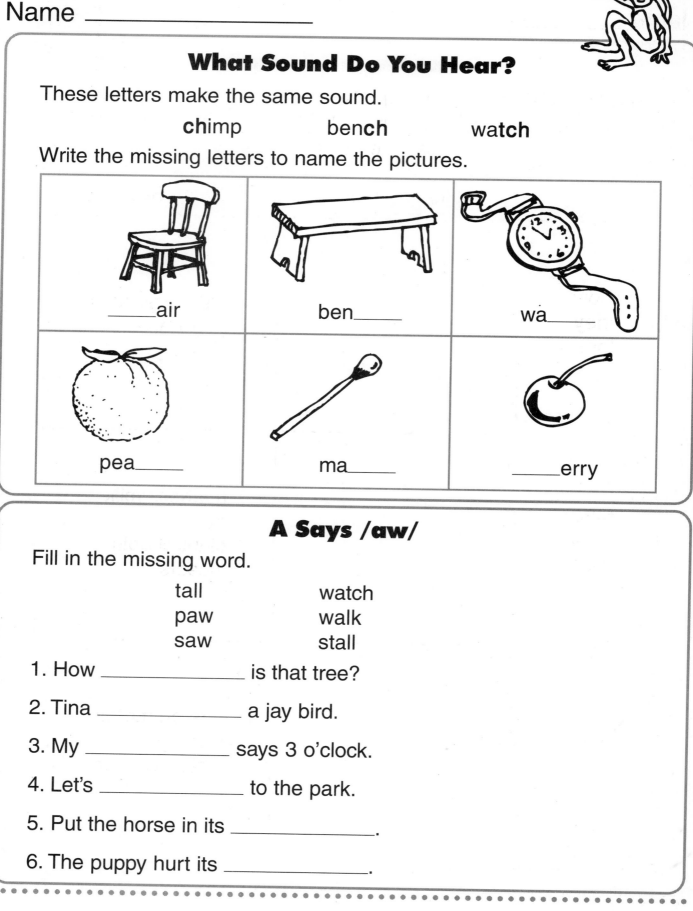

# What Sound Do You Hear?

These letters make the same sound.

**ch**imp          ben**ch**          wa**tch**

Write the missing letters to name the pictures.

_____air          ben_____          wa_____

pea_____          ma_____          _____erry

# A Says /aw/

Fill in the missing word.

| | |
|---|---|
| tall | watch |
| paw | walk |
| saw | stall |

1. How _____ is that tree?

2. Tina _____ a jay bird.

3. My _____ says 3 o'clock.

4. Let's _____ to the park.

5. Put the horse in its _____.

6. The puppy hurt its _____.

Name _____

# Babies

Jane Goodall's son was born in Tanzania. He grew up surrounded by chimpanzees that lived there. Fill in the chart comparing a human baby and a chimpanzee baby.

|  | Human Baby | Chimp Baby |
|---|---|---|
| How they look |  | like a little adult<br>very hairy |
| What they eat |  | mother's milk<br>fruit<br>plant shoots<br>insects |
| What they do |  | ride on mother<br>play<br>watch and learn |

Read and Understand Grade 2 EMC 639

# Answer Key

**Note:** The answers to some comprehension questions are given in complete sentences; some answers are not in complete sentences. The level of your students will determine whether you require that answers be in the form of complete sentences.

## Page 5
1. They had been fishing.
2. The flap of the tent was open.
3. A fox had made the mess.
4. He saw it wiggling.
5. The fox had Max's sox in its mouth.
6. He pulled Max away so the fox could get out.
   OR   ...so the fox wouldn't hurt Max.
7. He tied it so no more animals could get in.
8. Answers will vary.

## Page 6
1. Uncle Ted asked Max to get his jacket
2. Max saw that the tent flap was open.
3. The inside of the tent was a mess.
4. A fox peeked out of the sleeping bag.
5. Uncle Ted pulled Max out of the tent.
6. The fox ran out of the tent.

## Page 7
exit — to leave a place
visitor — someone who comes to see you
tent — a bedroom when you camp
sleeping bag — a warm bag to sleep in
flap — the opening into a tent
peek — look
jacket — something to wear
laugh — a happy sound

sleeping bag, tent, jacket

## Page 8
| fox | box | sox |
| six | Max | mix |

| noon | | cook | |
|------|------|------|------|
| moon | hoop | took | hood |
| bloom | boot | stood | book |
| school | food | wood | shook |

## Page 9

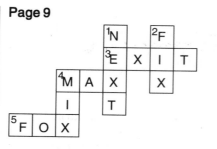

The fox is in a <u>sleeping bag</u>.
It has one of Max's <u>sox</u> in its mouth.
The fox ripped open <u>the bread</u>.

## Page 11
1. They said "Eeek!" OR They screamed.
2. grasshopper <u>jump high</u>
   bumblebee <u>collect pollen</u>
   cricket <u>rub wings together to chirp</u>
3. A beetle has hard wing covers.
4. A bug has a long tube to suck juice with.
5. Answers will vary.

## Page 12
1. grasshopper — Susan
2. beetle — Yolanda
3. cricket — Carlos
4. bumblebee — Harry
5. bug — all the children

| Insects | People | Plants |
|---------|--------|--------|
| grasshopper | Susan | tree |
| ant | Carlos | bush |
| moth | Maria | vine |
| bug | Harry | flower |
| cricket | Yolanda | weed |

## Page 13
said
yelled
howled
shouted
cried
explained

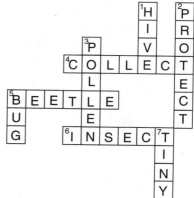

## Page 14
| 1. i | 6. e |
|------|------|
| 2. i | 7. i |
| 3. e | 8. e |
| 4. e | 9. e |
| 5. e | 10. i |

<u>e</u>
<u>i</u>

bumblebee - orange
cricket - green
grasshopper - orange
bug - red
beetle - green
ant - red

## Page 15
1. three parts
2. antennae
3. six legs

Read and Understand Grade 2 EMC 639

**Page 17**
1. The messenger brought a box from Uncle Wilber.
2. Uncle Wilber sent Oscar so Sarah and Sid could take care of him while Uncle Wilber was gone.
3. They kept Oscar a week.
4. Uncle Wilber gave them a box that made a hissing sound.
5. Answers will vary.
6. You never knew what Uncle Wilber would send you.
Pictures will vary.

**Page 18**
A messenger came with a box.
A goldfish in a bowl was in the box.
Sarah and Sid took care of Oscar.
Uncle Wilber came on Friday.
Uncle Wilber left a thank-you present.
Something in the box hissed.

**Page 19**
messenger — words sent from one person to another
message — a tap on the door
strange — a present
knock — a person that brings messages
gift — different

wet paint        keep off the grass
this side up      stop

**Page 20**
knob      knife      knight
knee      knot      knit

Answers may vary. Possible compound words include:
goldfish, cowboy, cowgirl, buttercup, pancake, cupcake, applesauce

**Page 21**
It is her birthday.
new shoes
a brush and paints
a baseball mitt
a pet puppy

**Page 23**
1. Grandfather liked to work in his garden.
2. Grandfather grew carrots.
3. He couldn't pull out the giant carrot.
4. He asked for help. OR Grandmother and the animals helped him.
5. Answers will vary.

**Page 24**
1. Grandfather grew carrots in his garden.
2. Grandfather saw a giant carrot.
3. Grandfather pulled very hard. The carrot did not come out.
4. Grandfather, Grandmother, the cat, and the mouse all pulled.
5. And the carrot came out!

**Page 25**
1. peas      2. corn      3. beet
4. carrot      5. spinach      6. celery

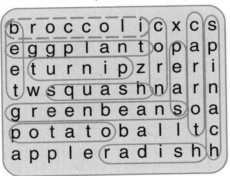

**Page 26**
Tom      pull      car
had      egg      pick
to      the      tug
fill      ten      apple
are      see      is
mine      up      hot
ask      beg      over
under      off      mule

(answers may be in a different order)
carrot
vegetable
Grandfather
Grandmother
garden
top
rows
cat
mouse

**Page 27**
Answers will vary.

**Page 30**
1. There were three goats.
2. The troll lived under the bridge.
3. The little goat got the troll to wait for a bigger brother.
4. The big goat hit the troll so hard he wasn't seen again.
5. The troll was gone so they could go across the bridge.

✓ A goat can talk.
✗ A goat can eat green grass.
✗ A goat can walk across a bridge.
✓ A goat can hit a troll.
✗ A goat can be little or big.

**Page 31**
3        1
4        6
2        5

**Page 32**
1. bridge
2. crooked
3. beg
4. troll
5. second
6. growl

The goats ate grass — on the hillside.
A bad troll wanted — to eat the goats.
The goats went — across the bridge.
"Try to eat me," — said the little goat.
The troll jumped out — and shouted at the goat.
"Wait for my brother," — said Big Billy Goat Gruff.

**Page 33**
bridge    troll    grass
grapes    train    broom

1. taller
2. tallest
3. biggest
4. colder
5. fastest

**Page 34**

bad          big eyes
lazy         handsome
long nose   hungry
mean       funny
friendly     scary

Answers will vary.
Pictures will vary.

**Page 36**

1. small, furry, twitchy whiskers, black eyes
2. Hammy lives in a cage.
3. dry pet food, fruit, vegetables, seeds, hamburger
4. The hamster will bite if it is scared or tired.
5. Answers will vary - could be... They watch him care for Hammy. They see him feed the hamster, clean its cage, and pet it.
6. Answers will vary.

(run through tubes)   fly a kite
(stuff its cheeks
with food)         (sleep)
sing a song      (drink water)
(eat)          draw a picture
ride a bike      (tear up paper)

**Page 37**

Answers will vary - could be...
1. feed it
2. give it water
3. keep its cage clean
4. pet it
5. give it toys

Pictures will vary

**Page 38**

1. hamster
2. cage
3. twitchy
4. hamburger
5. tear
6. wheel

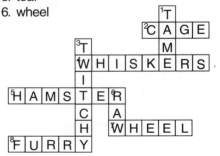

**Page 39**

1. bite
2. can
3. cake
4. bit
5. cane
6. cage
7. tub
8. tame

1. k
2. s
3. s
4. k
5. k
6. s
7. s
8. k
9. k
10. s

**Page 40**

**Page 42**

1. Maggie wanted a kite that she made herself.
2. paper, wood, glue, string
3. to keep her brother out
4. any reasonable answer
5. any reasonable answer
6. Answers will vary.

1. ☺     5. ☹
2. ☺     6. ☹
3. ☹     7. ☺
4. ☺     8. ☹

**Page 43**

Picture should show Maggie building her kite.
Picture should show the kite in the tree.
Pictures will vary.

**Page 44**

1. a
2. c
3. a
4. c
5. a
Pictures will vary.

**Page 45**

string    straw
strong   street
stripes   stranger

1. straw
2. stripes
3. stranger
4. street
5. strong
6. string

1. i      8. a
2. i      9. i
3. o     10. u
4. a    11. o
5. o    12. e
6. i     13. a
7. e    14. e

**Page 46**

```
m o w e d g o t r t d
r b w a r a c e d o l
a u e b i l l d r o o
n y n m a d e z x k c
b o t g i r l h a d k
s a i d r w o r k e d
```

Answers will vary - could be...
They are made of paper.
They have strings.
They fly in the sky.

Answer will vary - could be...
They are different shapes.
They are different sizes.
The strings are in different places.

## Page 48
1. Unpopped corn is hard and yellow. Cooked popcorn is fluffy and white.
2. The water turns to steam.
3. The steam pushes the hard cover until it breaks.
4. It pops open when it gets hot.

## Page 49
Get out the oil.
Pour some in the pot.

Plop go the kernels.
Now, wait until it's hot.

Pop goes the first kernel.
Pop goes the next.

Then pop, pop...explosion.
There go all the rest.

Pictures should reflect the poem verse.

## Page 50
1. water and melon
2. pea and nut
3. cow and girl
4. base and ball
5. butter and cup
6. pan and cake

## Page 51
then   think   there
thin   their   thorn
thank  that    thing

1. there
2. thin
3. thorn
4. then
5. think
6. that
Answers will vary

## Page 52
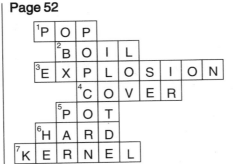
The mystery word is <u>popcorn</u>.

## Page 55
1. She lived in Athens. OR She lived in Greece.
2. It was her Name Day too. OR To wish her Happy Name Day.
3. She took candy.
4. It was at Grandmother's house.
5. Answers will vary - could be... There was music, food, friends, and singing.
6. It had been a present to Grandmother from her mother.
7. There are good things to eat. There are gifts. There are people having fun.

Answers will vary

## Page 56
Order of sentences:
4
3
2
6
1
5

Order of pictures:
4   1
3   2

## Page 57
1. classmates
2. whisper
3. candy
4. Athens
5. celebrate
6. sparkle

1. Eleni's (bracelet)
2. Sam's (bike)
3. Raul's (dog)
4. Ann's (book)
5. Lee's (hat)
6. Will's (ball)

## Page 58
| ed | d | t |
|---|---|---|
| wanted | lived | looked |
| lifted | named | dressed |
| shouted | filled | jumped |
| painted | sparkled | boxed |

1. were
2. was
3. was
4. were
5. were
6. was

## Page 59
Answers will vary.

## Page 61
1. a lion and a mouse
2. The mouse ran across the lion's paw.
3. The lion was in a hunter's net.
4. The mouse gnawed the ropes to free the lion.
5. Answers will vary - could be... He wasn't hungry He thought the mouse was funny. He was a kind lion.
6. The lion had let him go.

## Page 62
1. The mouse was caught.
2. The lion let the mouse go.
3. The lion was caught.
4. The mouse let the lion go.

The lion was...
   large
   loud
   unhappy
The mouse was...
   small
   brave
   hungry
They both were...
   helpful
   trapped
   in danger

**Page 63**

lunch      net      gnaw
king of beasts   shade   hunter
Answers will vary, but must contain
the words listed above.

**Page 64**

1. laughed    laughing
2. looked     looking
3. roared     roaring

1. napped     napping
2. begged     begging
3. trapped    trapping

1. napping
2. begged
3. roared
4. trapped
5. looking

**Page 65**

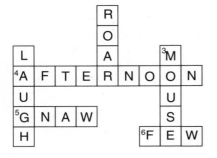

I found __7__ mice.

**Page 68**

1. He went to a farm.
2. Connie and Jacob went with him.
3. jeep  pickup  hay wagon  train  horse
4. Dad ask him to see that the children got off the train in Dayton. OR ...to see they meet Mr. Porter
5. Answers will vary - could be... He was surprised. OR He was excited. He had fun at the farm. The surprise party was fun. He liked the train ride with his friends.

Mother
Jacob
Mr. Porter
Ray
Dad

**Page 69**

best ——— don't start yet
wait ——— a kind of wall around a yard
slow poke ——— most good
conductor ——— someone who is not fast
fence ——— in charge of people on a train

1. fence
2. conductor
3. slow poke
4. best
5. wait

1. aren't    4. don't
2. I'll      5. it's
3. let's    6. can't

**Page 70**

1. "Wake up, Ray. It's time to get up," said Mother.
2. While Ray was eating breakfast, Connie and Jacob came in.
3. Dad drove the children to the train.
4. The children had fun painting the fence.
5. Ray, Connie, and Jacob rode in the hay wagon.
6. A surprise birthday party was set up by the lake. Ray had a good time.

**Page 71**

c<u>a</u>ke   h<u>ay</u>   r<u>ai</u>n
cl<u>ay</u>   p<u>ai</u>nt   sk<u>ate</u>

**Page 72**

Answers will vary.

**Page 74**

1. a goat
2. any three of these: clay, moss, labels, hay, leaves, greasy pans, socks, beans and peas
3. anything is a good lunch
4. because of the things he eats
5. Answers will vary.

Pictures will vary.

**Page 75**

1. get
2. clay
3. munch
4. socks
5. pans
6. peas

1. Answers will vary
2. Answers will vary
3. Answers will vary
4. Answers will vary

ck    c
ck    k
k     c
k     ck

**Page 76**

pet ——— the meal we eat in the middle of the day
lunch ——— an animal you care for and love
moss ——— a paper on a can or jar that tells what is in it
label ——— small soft green plants that grow on rocks and trees
munch ——— has grease or oil on it
greasy ——— to nibble on food

1. she'll    3. I'll
2. we'll    4. they'll

Answers will vary.

**Page 77**

Good for Lunch
1. sandwich
2. milk
3. soup
4. apple
5. chicken
6. cookie
Not for Lunch
1. bed
2. sock
3. grass
4. box
5. mitten
6. mouse

Pictures will vary.

## Page 78

(green grass) (hay) ~~Grandpa's socks~~

(leaves on trees) (apples) ~~tin can~~

~~bedroom slipper~~ ~~little rocks~~ (carrot sticks)

## Page 80

1. There were playing in the backyard.
2. There weren't any cookies in the jar. OR The cookies were all gone.
3. got the recipe
   read the recipe
   took the cookies out of the oven
4. So they will know how to make the food.
5. Answers will vary.

## Page 81

3
1
6
4
2
7
5

Mark — "You need a recipe."
      "Making cookies is hard work!"
      "I want a snack."
Mom — "Just a minute."
      "What are ingredients?"
Art — "Let's make some."

## Page 82

Crossword:
1. B
2. D
3. R
4. OATMEAL (O-A-T-M-E-A-L)
   OUGH (down from O)
   RECIPE (down from R)
   BOWL (down from B)
5. MIX
6. OVEN

Answers will vary.

## Page 83

jar    card
star   car

1. clean
2. cold
3. big
4. found
5. out
6. long
7. happy
8. wet

## Page 84

**Fill the Cookie Jar**

Answers will vary.

## Page 87

1. old woman, old man, cat, dog
2. Her husband liked gingerbread.
3. She was surprised.
4. He couldn't get over the river.
5. He got the gingerbread man to climb on his head and then the fox ate it.
6. Answers will vary - could be...
   Gingerbread men can't run.
   Gingerbread men can't talk.
   A fox doesn't eat gingerbread men.

Pictures will vary.

## Page 88

2
4
1
5
3
6
7

**People**
1. old woman
2. farmer
3. old man

**Animals**
1. cat and dog
2. fox
3. horse and cow

Answers will vary - could be...
The gingerbread man is not a person or an animal.
A gingerbread man is something to eat.

## Page 89

1. c
2. b
3. b
4. a
5. c
6. tiny, wee, small

they - cat and dog
she - old woman
he - farmer
it - gingerbread man

Read and Understand Grade 2 EMC 639

## Page 90

Answers will vary but must be real words containing "old."

1. j      5. j
2. g      6. j
3. g      7. g
4. g      8. j

## Page 91

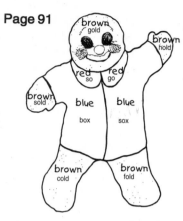

## Page 93

1. all his life
2. she is very old
3. she makes him brownies and reads to him
4. Gregor is the best neighbor. He and Jamal are friends.
5. Answers will vary - could be...
   His neighbors are helpful.
   He has known them all his life.
   He likes his neighbors.

1. Mr. Brown
2. Dr. Ramirez
3. Aunt Rose
4. Gregor's dad
5. Mrs. Brown
6. Gregor

## Page 94

## Page 95

1. neighbors
2. brownies
3. cane
4. porch
5. gorilla
6. camp out
7. pack
8. blew

Pictures will vary.

## Page 96

eight   weigh   neighbor
Sentences will vary.

1. blew
2. read
3. buy
4. weigh
5. ate
6. blue
7. way
8. eight

## Page 97

Answers will vary

## Page 100

1. Frog eggs look like jelly.
2. A frog's skin lets in water.
3. Frogs sit and wait and catch food with a sticky tongue.
4. Webbed feet help the frog swim.
5. Tadpoles have gills like fish.
6. Tadpoles eat little plants called algae.
7. Tree frogs have sticky feet for climbing trees.
   Pond frogs have webbed feet for swimming.

frog eggs     tadpoles     frog

## Page 101

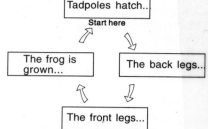

## Page 102

1. toad
2. frog
3. amphibians
4. gills
5. moist
6. algae
7. burrows

## Page 103

1. boil   3. oil   5. soil
2. toy    4. Roy   6. moist

1. boil
2. toy
3. moist
4. oil
5. Roy
6. soil

1. small     5. large
2. smile     6. shout
3. moist     7. glad
4. quick     8. slow

## Page 104

1. yes
2. yes
3. no
4. yes
5. yes
6. yes
7. no
8. yes
9. yes
10. no
11. yes

Picture of a snake.

Read and Understand Grade 2 EMC 639